W. S Weeden, Leonard Weaver, J. W Van de Venter

Gospel Songs of Grace and Glory

W. S Weeden, Leonard Weaver, J. W Van de Venter

Gospel Songs of Grace and Glory

ISBN/EAN: 9783743351196

Manufactured in Europe, USA, Canada, Australia, Japa

Cover: Foto ©Thomas Meinert / pixelio.de

Manufactured and distributed by brebook publishing software (www.brebook.com)

W. S Weeden, Leonard Weaver, J. W Van de Venter

Gospel Songs of Grace and Glory

GOSPEL SONGS

⁂ OF ⁂

GRACE and GLORY.

EDITED BY

W. S. WEEDEN,   LEONARD WEAVER
and J. W. VAN DE VENTER

WITH

Contributions, Old and New, from Many of the Most Widely Known Song Writers and Composers.

⁂

PUBLISHED BY THE

SEBRING PUBLISHING CO.,

441 Pearl St., New York City, N. Y.

Copyright, 1896, by Geo. E. Sebring.

PREFACE.

IN compiling "**Gospel Songs of Grace and Glory**," the editors have kept in mind the fact that all Evangelists and aggressive Christian workers, find that in a song book, to be of permanent use in soul winning, two things at least are needed.

Music that can be sung by the masses, and words that shall set forth the Gospel Message in such a manner as to awaken response in the inner depths of the soul.

The briefest review of "**Gospel Songs of Grace and Glory**" will show that this book will meet every need for such work. Like "**Sparkling Gems**," "**Sweet as Honey**," from the "**Rock of Ages**," these songs will drop from the lips of thousands, lifting heart and thought above this sin-blighted earth to **Him** who came in **Grace to** "**bring many sons to Glory**."

We desire to acknowledge our obligations to **A. J. Showalter, H. N. Lincoln, W. A. Ogden, M. L. McPhail**, and many others for their kindness shown us in our work.

NOTICE.—The words and music of nearly every piece in this book are copyright property and must not be reprinted in any form whatever without the written permission of the authors.

THE PUBLISHERS.

Gospel Songs of Grace and Glory.

1. Then Sing the Songs.

J. W. Van Deventer. W. S. Weeden.

1. The gos-pel songs of sav-ing grace, The blessed songs of glo-ry,
2. They speak in tones of ten-der love, Of man-y sins for-giv-en;
3. They strengthen us up-on the way, And help us in our sor-row;
4. They tell us of a land of gold, Where mortals do not sev-er;

They bring sal-va-tion to the race, Pro-claim the old, old sto-ry.
They bring the pow-er from a-bove, And lift us near-er heav-en.
They fill with joy each pass-ing day, And cheer us for the mor-row.
Where saints a-bide and ne'er grow old, Where we shall live for-ev-er.

CHORUS.

Then sing the songs with cho-rus grand, The songs of grace and glo-ry,

Un-til the lost of ev-'ry land, Has heard the old, old sto-ry.

Copyright, 1896, by Weeden & Van DeVenter.

Sing On. Concluded.

My heart is fill'd with rapture, My soul is lost in praise.

Sing on; O bliss-ful music, With ev-'ry note you raise,
Sing on; bliss-ful, bliss-ful music,

My heart is fill'd with rapture, My soul is lost in praise.

3. Arlington. C. M.

DR. ARNE.

1. Am I a soldier of the cross, A follower of the Lamb?
2. Must I be carried to the skies On flow'ry beds of ease?

And shall I fear to own His cause, Or blush to speak His name?
While others fought to win the prize, And sail'd thro' bloody seas?

3 Are there no foes for me to face?
  Must I not stem the flood?
  Is this vile world a friend to grace,
  To help me on to God?

4 Since I must fight, if I would reign;
  Increase my courage, Lord;
  I'll bear the toil, endure the pain,
  Supported by Thy word.

5. Oh, such Wonderful Love!

I. N. McHose. Alt. I. N. McHose.

1. O the great love the dear Sav-ior has shown To shameful-ly die on the tree, Leaving his sceptre and beau-ti-ful throne, To res-cue a sin-ner like me!
2. Pal-ac-es, mansions and inns had no room For Christ, who so joy-ful-ly came Down from yon heaven our path to il-lume, And save us from sin and from shame.
3. Man of great sorrows and homeless was He, But yet my Re-deemer and Friend, Pouring in in-fi-nite streams up-on me, A love that can nev-er-more end.

CHORUS.

Oh, ... such wonder-ful love! Oh, ... such wonder-ful love! Je-sus, my Sav-ior, left sceptre and throne, To res-cue a sinner like me.

Oh, such wonder-ful,

By per. HENRY DATE, owner of Copyright.

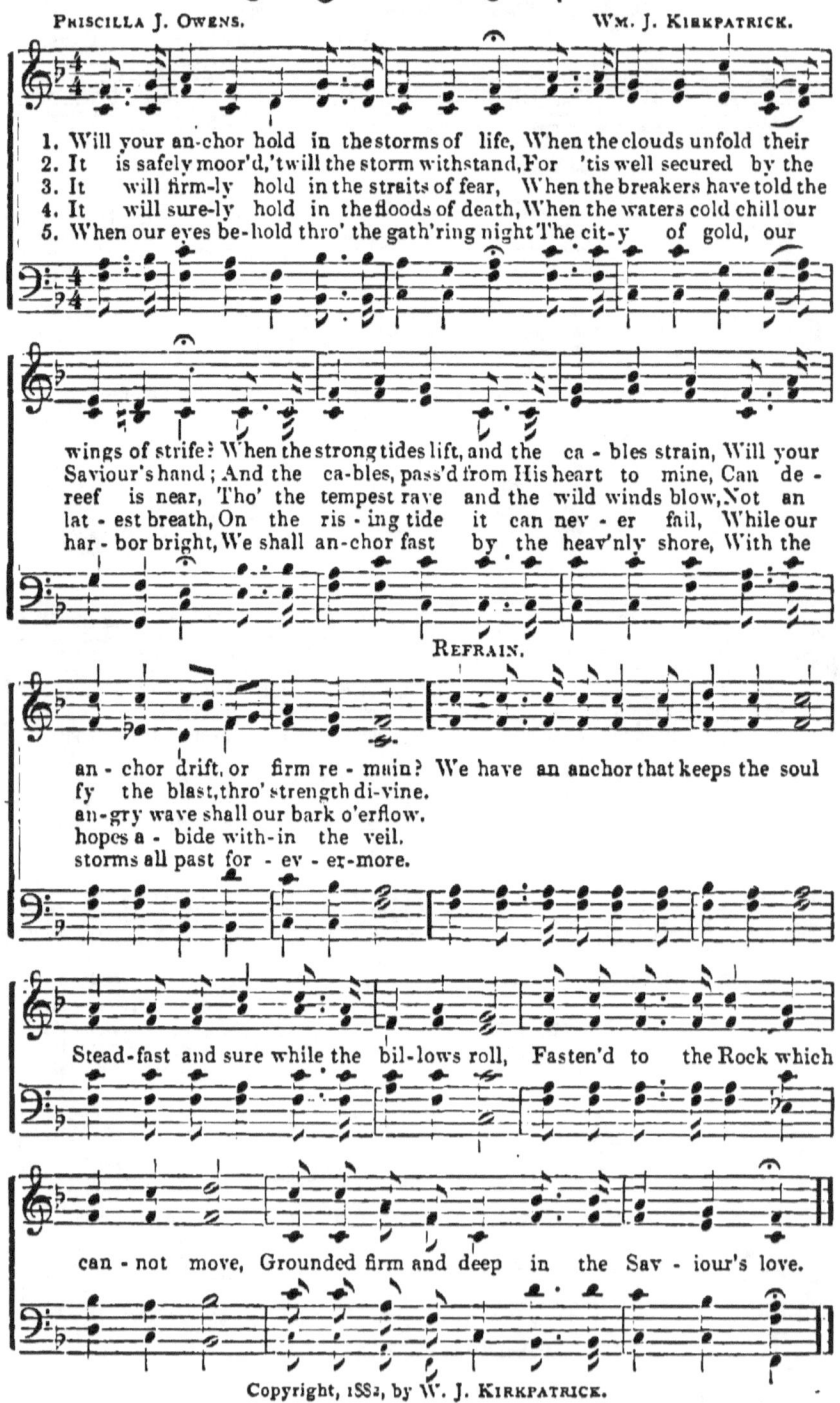

Meet Me There.

HENRIETTA E. BLAIR. WM. J. KIRKPATRICK.

1. On the hap-py, golden shore, Where the faithful part no more, When the storms of life are o'er, Meet me there ; Where the night dissolves away In-to pure and per-fect day, I am go-ing home to stay, Meet me there.
2. Here our fond-est hopes are vain, Dearest links are rent in twain ; But in heav'n no throb of pain, Meet me there ; By the riv-er sparkling bright, In the cit-y of de-light, Where our faith is lost in sight, Meet me there.
3. Where the harps of an-gels ring, And the blest for-ev-er sing, In the pal-ace of the King, Meet me there ; Where in sweet communion blend Heart with heart, and friend with friend, In a world that ne'er shall end, Meet me there.

D.S.—hap-py gold-en shore, Where the faithful part no more, Meet me there.

CHORUS.

Meet me there, Meet me there, Where the tree of life is blooming, Meet me there ; When the storms of life are o'er, On the Meet me there ;

Copyright of Wm. J. Kirkpatrick. Used by permission.

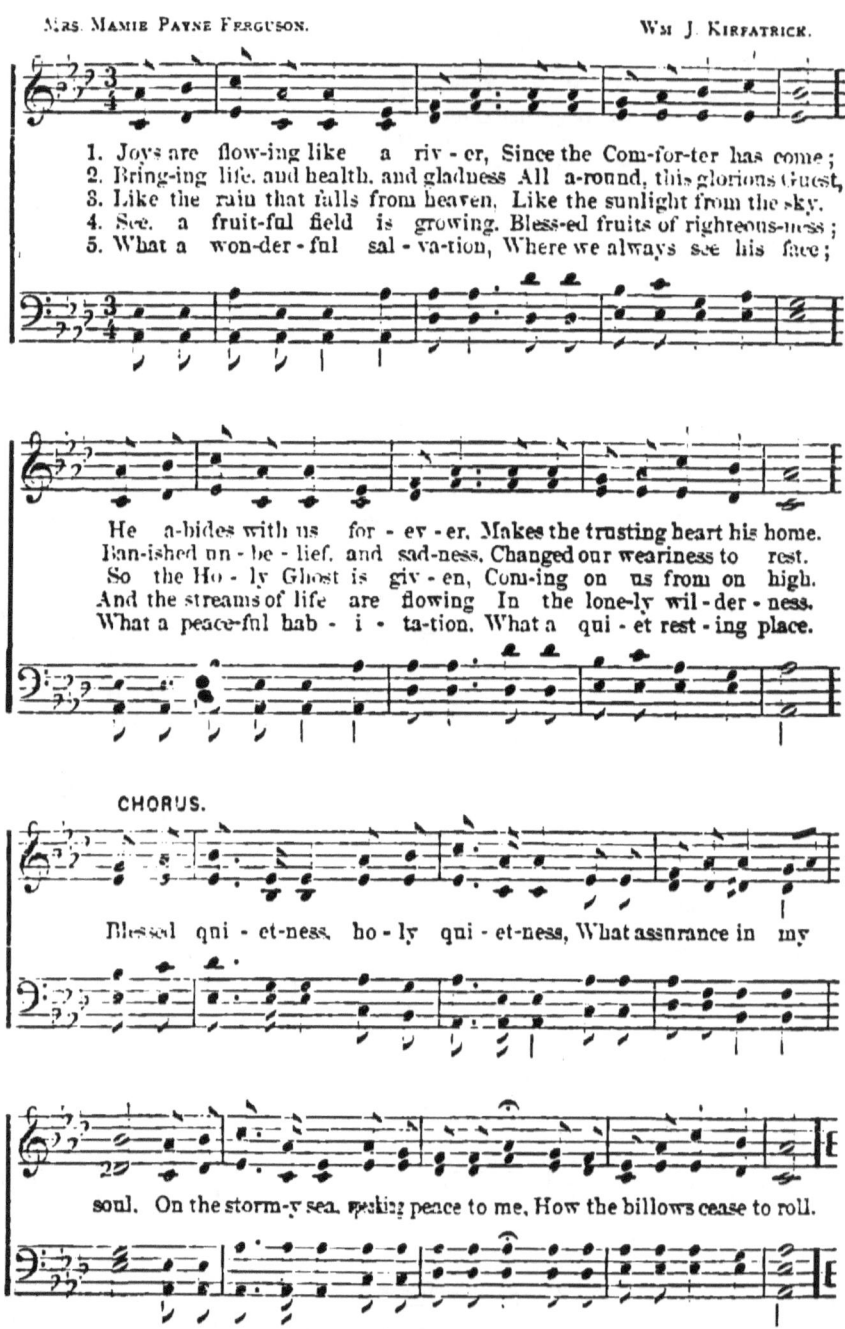

The General Roll Call.

J. W. Van DeVenter. W. S. Weeden.

1. When we see the King of kings appear In judgment on His throne, When the
2. When the na-tions of the earth shall hear The summons of the King, When the
3. Let us work un-til the Master comes, The time may not be long, 'Till we

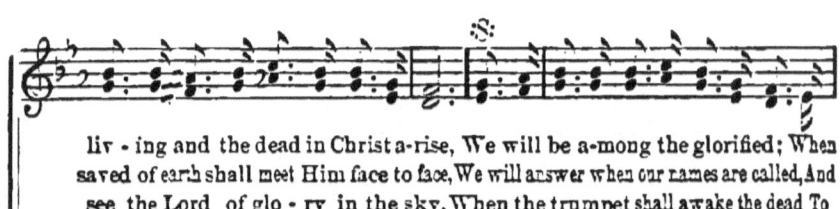

liv-ing and the dead in Christ a-rise, We will be a-mong the glorified; When
saved of earth shall meet Him face to face, We will answer when our names are called, And
see the Lord of glo-ry in the sky, When the trumpet shall awake the dead To

D. S.—*When our names are read up yonder, From the*

FINE.

Je-sus calls His own, When we gath-er to meet the Sav-ior in the skies.
praise Him as we sing Hal-le-lu-jah! for Je-sus sav'd us by His grace.
meet the coming throng, Oh, be read-y, the judgment day is draw-ing nigh.

pages white and fair, When the gen-er-al roll is called, we'll all be there.

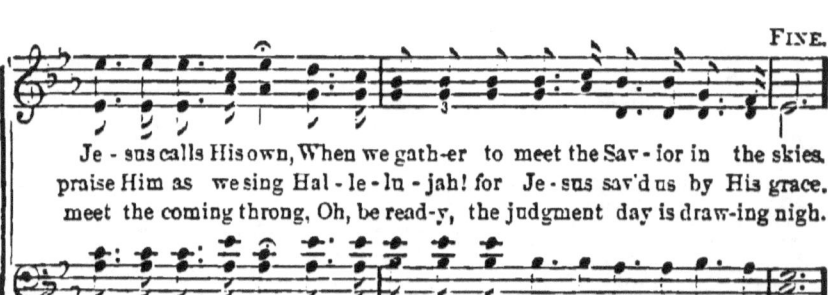

CHORUS. D. S.

You'll be there, I'll be there, On the res-ur-rec-tion morning we'll be there;

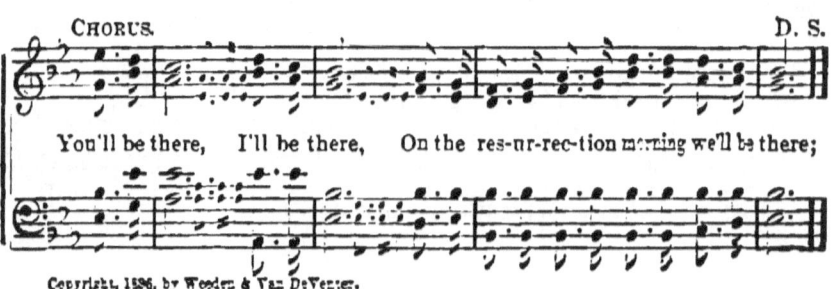

Copyright, 1896, by Weeden & Van DeVenter.

I Love to Tell the Story.—CONCLUDED.

To tell the old, old sto-ry, Of Je-sus and his love.

3 I love to tell the story!
'Tis pleasant to repeat
What seems, each time I tell it,
More wonderfully sweet.
I love to tell the story;
For some have never heard
The message of salvation
From God's own Holy Word.

4 I love to tell the story!
For those who know it best
Seem hungering and thirsting
To hear it like the rest.
And when, in scenes of glory,
I sing the *New, New Song*,
'Twill be the *Old, Old Story*,
That I have loved so long.

19 Sing Upon the Way.

"The ransomed of the Lord shall come to Zion with songs."—ISA. xxxv: 10.

THOMAS McKELLAR.   J. J. LOWE.

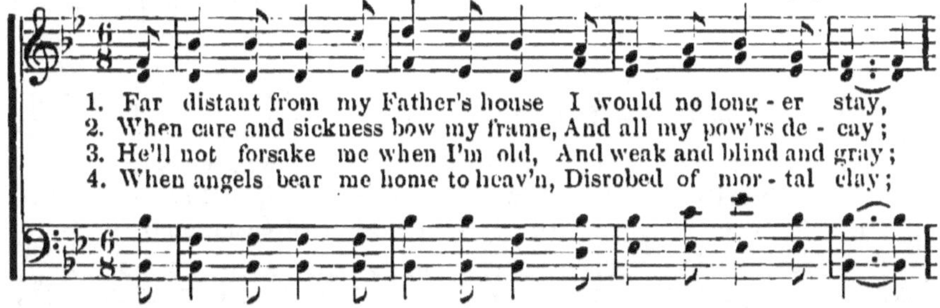

1. Far distant from my Father's house I would no long-er stay,
2. When care and sickness bow my frame, And all my pow'rs de-cay;
3. He'll not forsake me when I'm old, And weak and blind and gray;
4. When angels bear me home to heav'n, Disrobed of mor-tal clay;

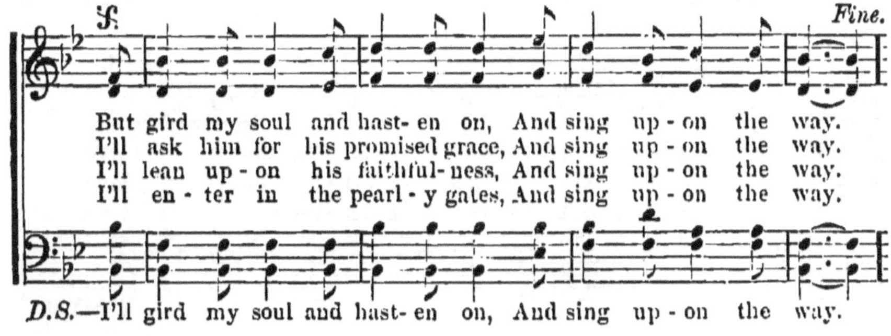

Fine.

But gird my soul and hast-en on, And sing up-on the way.
I'll ask him for his promised grace, And sing up-on the way.
I'll lean up-on his faithful-ness, And sing up-on the way.
I'll en-ter in the pearl-y gates, And sing up-on the way.

D.S.—I'll gird my soul and hast-en on, And sing up-on the way.

CHORUS.   *D.S.*

And sing up-on the way,.... And sing up-on the way;

Copyright, 1896, by W. S. Weeden.

Wonderful Story of Love. Concluded.

Won - der - ful!
Won - der-ful sto-ry of love: won-der-ful sto-ry of love!

21. Onward, Christian Soldiers!

SABINE BARING-GOULD.   Tune, "Onward." 6, 5.

1. On-ward, Christian sol-diers! Marching as to war, With the cross of Je-sus Go-ing on be-fore; Christ, the roy-al Mas-ter, Leads a-gainst the foe; For-ward in-to bat-tle, See, His ban-ners go!
2. Like a might-y ar-my Moves the Church of God; Brothers, we are tread-ing Where the saints have trod; We are not di-vid-ed, All one bod-y we; One in hope and doctrine, One in char-i-ty.
3. Crowns and thrones may perish, Kingdoms rise and wane, But the Church of Je-sus Con-stant will re-main; Gates of hell can nev-er 'Gainst that Church prevail: We have Christ's own promise, And that cannot fail.
4. On-ward, then, ye peo-ple! Join our hap-py throng, Blend with ours your voi-ces In the tri-umph song; Glo-ry, laud, and hon-or, Un-to Christ the King, This thro' countless a-ges Men and an-gels sing.

CHORUS.

Onward, Christian soldiers! Marching as to war, With the cross of Jesus Going on be - fore.

The Penitent's Plea.—Concluded.

sin a-way, Pow'r to keep me sinless day by day, For me, for me!
sin a-way, Pow'r to keep me sin - less day by day, For me, for me, for me!

Why Are You Waiting?

E. A. H.
Rev. Elisha A. Hoffman.

1. Why are you wait-ing, broth-er? Why do you still de - lay?
2. Why are you wait-ing, broth-er? Why is your heart so cold?
3. Why are you wait-ing, broth-er? Why still un - rec - on - ciled?
4. Why are you wait-ing, broth-er? Je - sus is ver - y near,

En - ter the door of mer - cy; Come, and be saved to - day.
Why not re - turn, re - pent - ant, In - to the Sav - ior's fold?
This is God's time of mer - cy; Trust Him, and be His child.
Bless-ing and sav - ing oth - ers, Read - y to save you here.

CHORUS.

Why are you waiting? Why are you waiting? Now is the gracious hour!

Why are you waiting? Why are you waiting? Now He will save with pow'r.

By permission of the Hoffman Music Co.

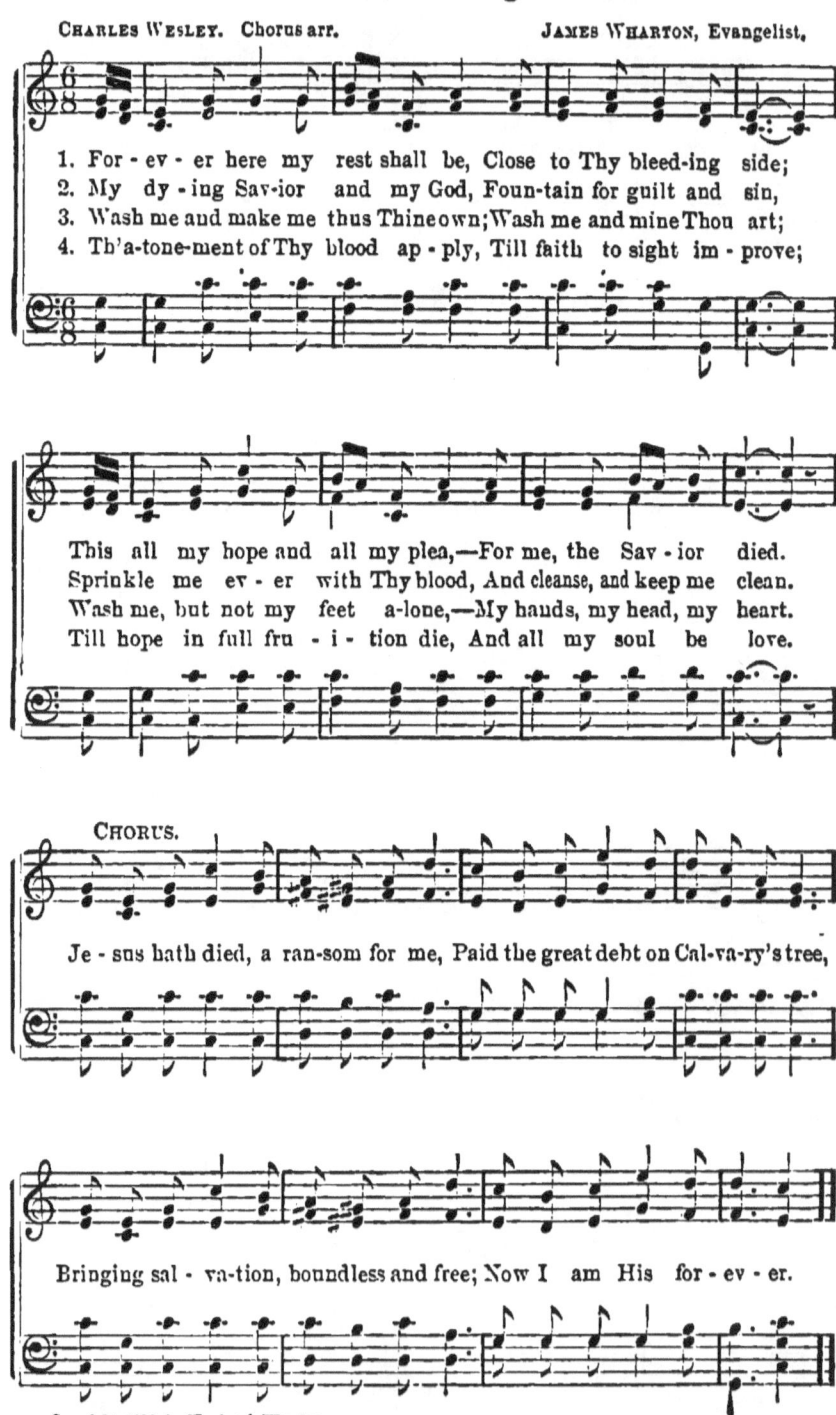

The Holy Ghost Has Fallen.—Concluded.

feel the mighty pow - er In pen - te - cost - al flame, Oh glo - ry, hal - le - lu - jah to the Sav - ior's name!

31 We'll Work till Jesus Comes. Dr. Miller.

1. O land of rest, for thee I sigh, When will the moment come,
When I shall lay my ar-mor by, And dwell in peace.......... at home?
2. No tranquil joys on earth I know, No peaceful, shelt'ring dome,
This world's a wil-der-ness of woe, This world is not my ...... my home.
3. To Je-sus Christ I fled for rest; He bade me cease to roam,
And lean for suc-cor on His breast, And He'd conduct .... me home.

Chorus.

We'll work till Je-sus comes, We'll work till Je-sus comes,
We'll work till Je-sus comes, And we'll be gath-er'd home.

34. Hold Up the Light.

A number of years ago there lived a lady near Armour, South Dakota, who always kept a light in the window all night long. A neighbor asked why she did this, and she replied, "You know the way is so long from here to Mitchell and return, and your boy, or my boy, or some one may be overtaken by the darkness on these trackless prairies, and because some one may need a light, I keep one in the window."

Words and Music by EMMA POWERS CRANMER.

1. Hold up the light, The way is so dark; Hold up the light, Where crime's left its mark. The soul, once so pure, Is now stained with sin;
2. Hold up the light, A broth-er is lost, Hold up the light, What-ev - er the cost; Tell him of Je - sus, The Might-y to save,
3. May - be my boy Is out in the cold, May - be your boy Is not in the fold, Read - y to per - ish, No help with-in sight;

CHORUS.

Hold up the light And gather them in.
How He was victor o'er sin and the grave. } Hold up the light, Hold up the light,
Then, O my brother, Let's hold up the light.

Man-y a wan-der - er, Out in the night, Peer-ing thro' darkness, No

Copyright, 1894, by Emma Powers Cranmer.

36. There's a Great Day Coming.

W. L. T.
W. L. Thompson.

1. There's a great day com-ing, A great day com-ing, There's a great day coming by and by, When the saints and the sin-ners shall be part-ed right and left, Are you read-y for that day to come?
2. There's a bright day com-ing, A bright day com-ing, There's a bright day coming by and by, But its brightness shall on-ly come to them that love the Lord, Are you read-y for that day to come?
3. There's a sad day com-ing, A sad day com-ing, There's a sad day coming by and by, When the sin-ner shall hear his doom, "De-part, I know ye not!" Are you read-y for that day to come?

Chorus.

Are you read-y? are you read-y? Are you read-y for the judgment day? Are you ready? are you ready for the judgment day?

By permission of W. L. Thompson & Co., East Liverpool, O.

37. The Comforter Abides.

J. W. Van Deventer.   W. A. Ogden.

1. When friends grow old and prove untrue,—The world with scorn derides,—
2. When tempest-tossed by surging sea, When struggling with the tides,
3. When doubts appear and tempt the heart, And fear within me hides,
4. My heart is filled with Jesus' love, In Him my soul confides,

This hope returns to me anew, The Comforter abides.
There is a tho't that strengthens me, The Comforter abides.
This heav'nly Guest does not depart, The Comforter abides.
And while He pleads for me above, The Comforter abides.

REFRAIN.

The Comforter abides,.... The Comforter abides,....
           abides,   abides,

This hope returns to me anew, The Comforter abides.
There is a hope that strengthens me, The Comforter abides.
This heav'nly Guest does not depart, The Comforter abides.
While He atones for me above, The Comforter abides.

Copyright, 1896, by W. S. Weeden.

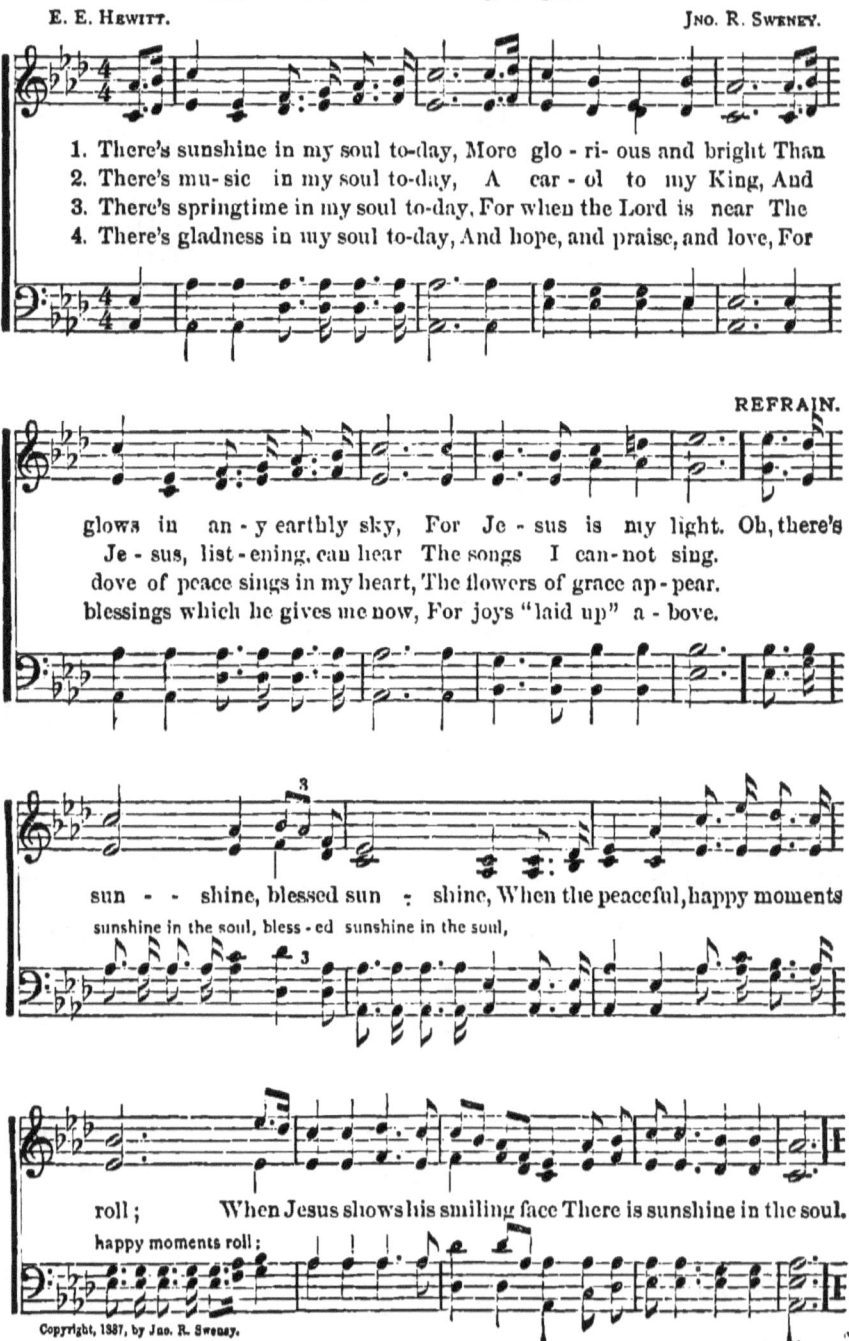

43. Master, Use Me.

E. A. H.   Rev. ELISHA A. HOFFMAN.

1. Send me forth, O bless-ed Master! where are souls in sorrow bowed, Send me forth to homes of want and homes of care, And with joy I will obey the call, and in Thy blessed name I will take the bless-ed light of the gos-pel there.
2. There are lives that may be brightened by a word of hope and cheer, There are souls with whom life's blessings I should share; There are hearts that may be lightened of the burdens which they bear; Let me take the blessed hope of the gos-pel there.
3. There is work within the vineyard, there is service to be done, There's a mes-sage of sal-va-tion to de-clare; Send me forth to tell the story to the homes of sin-ful men; Let me take the blessed Christ of the gos-pel there.
4. Oh, I would not be an i-dler in the vineyard of the Lord; With the Christ the vineyard-labor I would share; Into hearts that know not Jesus I would speak the sav-ing Word; Let me take the bless-ed joy of the gos-pel there.

D. S.—*read-y to re-port for or-ders,*
FINE.

CHORUS.—Call me forth.......... to act-ive serv - - - ice, Call me forth, call me forth, to act-ive serv-ice call me forth, And my prompt re-sponse shall be, "Here am I! send me;" I am *Mas-ter, sum-mon me, And I'll go on an-y er-rand of love for Thee.*

D. S.

Copyright, 1894, by the Hoffman Music Co.

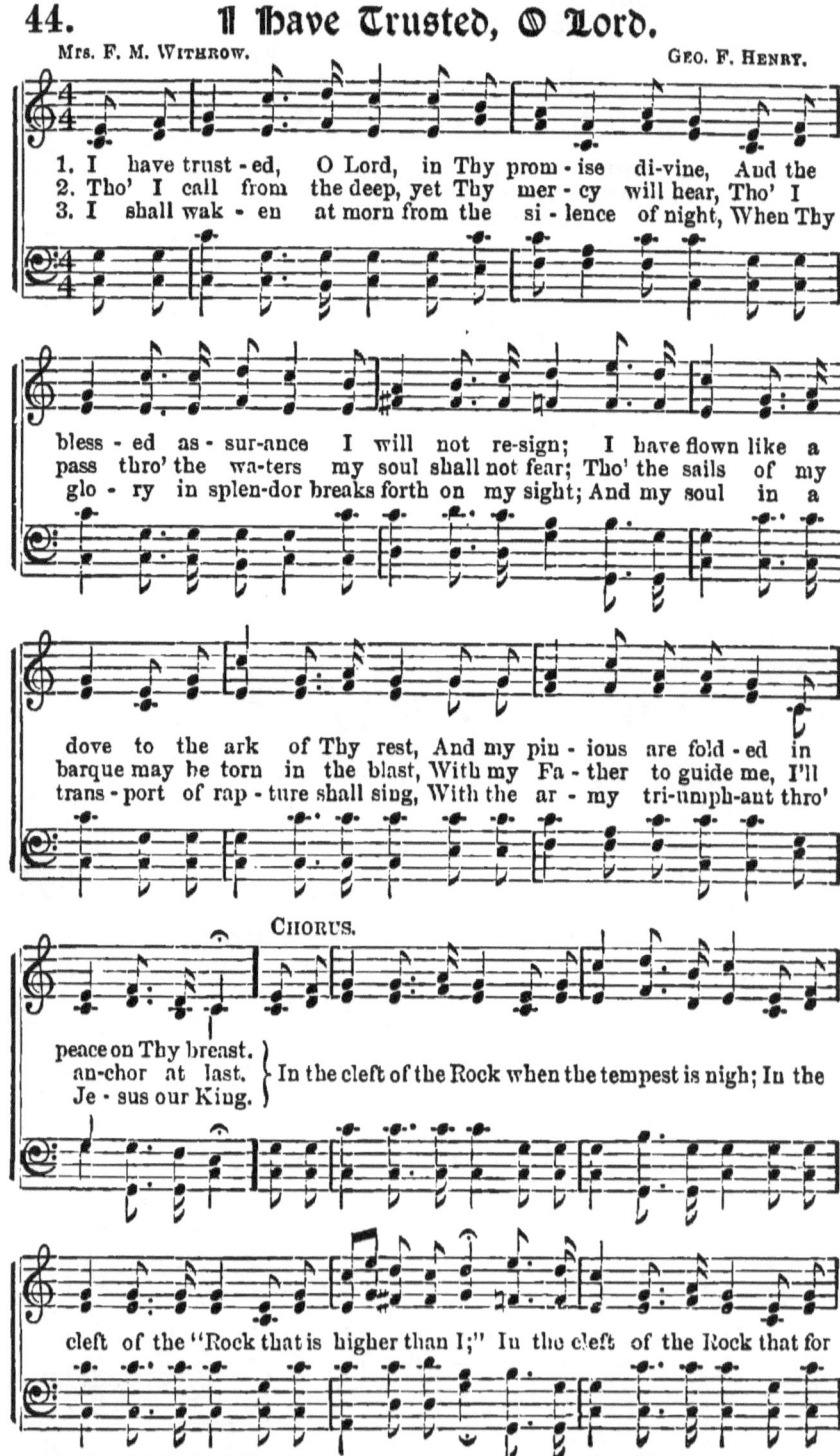

I Have Trusted, O Lord.—Concluded.

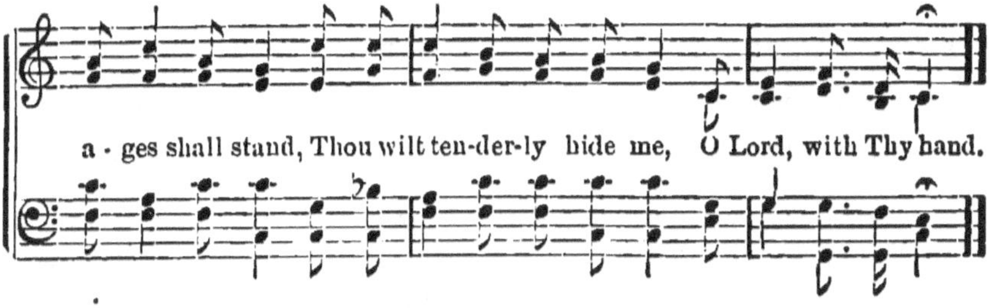

a - ges shall stand, Thou wilt ten-der-ly hide me, O Lord, with Thy hand.

45. That Blessed Hope.

Titus 2: 3.

G. A. WARBURTON. W. S. WEEDEN.

1. Im - pa-tient heart, be still, be still! What tho' He tar-ries long? What
2. My ea - ger heart, be still, be still! Thy Lord will surely come, And
3. My anxious heart, be still, be still! Watch, pray, and work, and then It

tho' the tri-umph song Is still de - layed? Thou hast His promise sure,
take thee to His home, With Him to dwell. It may not be to - day,
will not mat-ter when Thy Lord shall come. At mid-night or at noon,

And that is all se - cure, Be not a - fraid, be not a - fraid!
And yet, my soul, it may; I can - not tell, I can - not tell!
He can - not come too soon To take thee home, to take thee home!

Copyright, 1896, by W. S. Weeden.

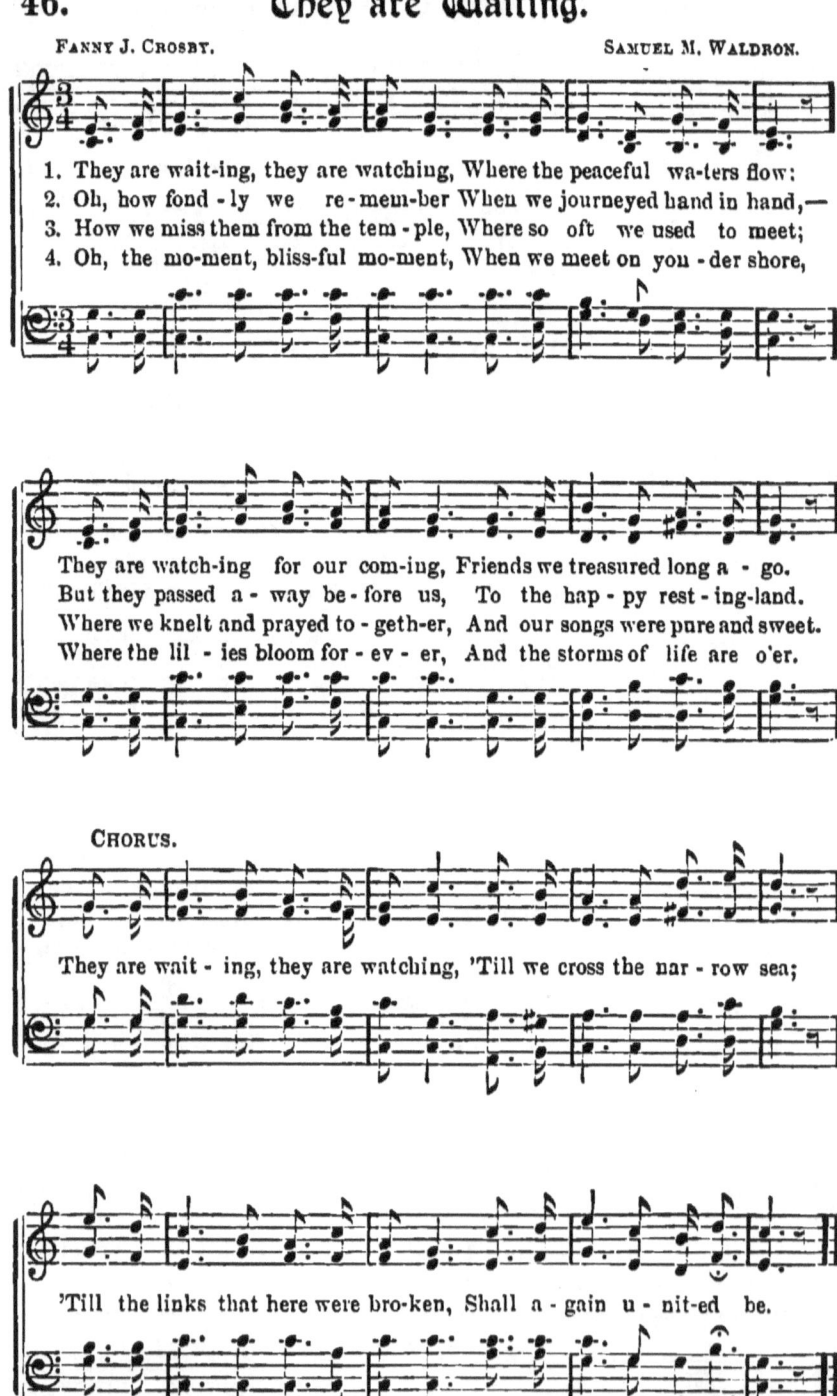

49. Listen to My Story.

J. W. Van De Venter.   S. C. Foster. Arr.

1. Down at the cross the Saviour found me, Weary of sin;
Then Jesus saw me, weak and weary, Came to my soul;
Darkness was ev'rywhere around me, Sorrow and gloom within.
Brought sunshine to my heart so dreary, Whisper'd, and I was whole.

CHORUS.
Listen, listen to my story: At His feet I bow;
He saves me, and He keeps me—glory! Praise the Lord! He saves me now!

2 He found me on a barren mountain,
   Hungry and cold;
He bro't me to the cleansing fountain,
   Placed me within the fold;
I know the Savior will protect me,
   Show me the way;
He never, never will neglect me,
   I shall not go astray.

3 He fills my heart to overflowing—
   Wonderful love!
Rich blessings He is now bestowing,
   Peace from the throne above.
Now when temptations great assail me,
   I can endure;
His grace and mercy never fail me,
   He makes His child secure.

Copyright, 1894, by J. W. Van De Venter.

3 Thou dying Lamb,:│ Thy ║: precious blood :║
Shall never lose its power,
Till all the ransomed ║: Church of God :║
Are saved, to sin no more.

4 E'er since by faith ║: I saw the stream :║
Thy flowing wounds supply,
Redeeming love ║: has been my theme,:║
And shall be till I die.

56. Jesus Is Passing This Way.

E. A. H.
J. H. T.

1. Is there a sin-ner a-wait-ing Mer-cy and pardon to-day?
2. Brother the M ster is wait-ing, Waiting to free-ly for-give;
3. Yes, he is coming to bless you While in contrition you bow;

Welcome the news that we bring him: "Jesus is passing this way!"
Why not this moment accept him, Trust in his grace and live?
Coming from sin to re-deem you, Read-y to save you now;

Coming in love and in mer - cy, Pardon and peace to be-stow,
He is so tender and pre - cious, He is so near you to - day;
Can you re-fuse the sal-va - tion Je - sus is of-fer-ing here?

Coming to save the poor sin - ner From his heart-anguish and woe.
O-pen your heart to receive him, While he is p ssing this way.
O-pen your heart to ad-mit him, While he is coming so near.

Chorus.

Je-sus is passing this way...... To - day,......... to - day,
Jesus is passing this way, To-day, is passing to - day!

Jesus is Passing This Way. Concluded.

While he is near, O be-lieve him, O-pen your heart to receive him, For

Je-sus is passing this way, this way, Is passing this way to-day.

57. Jesus Saves Me Now.

A. O. D.
Alt. fr. S. J. VAIL, by per.

Joyful.

1. { Je-sus hath died and hath ris-en a-gain, Pardon and peace to be-stow;
   { Ful-ly I trust Him; from sin's guilty stain, Je-sus saves me now;
2. { Sins condem-nation is o-ver and gone, Je-sus a-lone knoweth how;
   { Life and Sal-va-tion my soul hath put on: Je-sus saves me now.

D. C.—Je - sus saves me all the time; Je - sus saves me now,

CHORUS.

Je - sus saves me now; Je - sus saves me now; Yes,
He saves me now, He saves me now;

3 Satan may tempt, but he never shall reign,
   That Christ will never allow;
   Doubts I have buried, and this is my strain,
   " Jesus saves me now."

4 Resting in Jesus, abiding in Him,
   Gladly my faith can avow,—
   Never again need my pathway be dim:
   Jesus saves me now.

5 Jesus is stronger than Satan and sin,
   Satan to Jesus must bow;
   Therefore I triumph without and with-
   Jesus saves me now.   [in:

6 Sorrow and pain may beset me about,
   Nothing can darken my brow;
   Battl'ing in faith, I can joyfully shout;
   " Jesus saves me now."

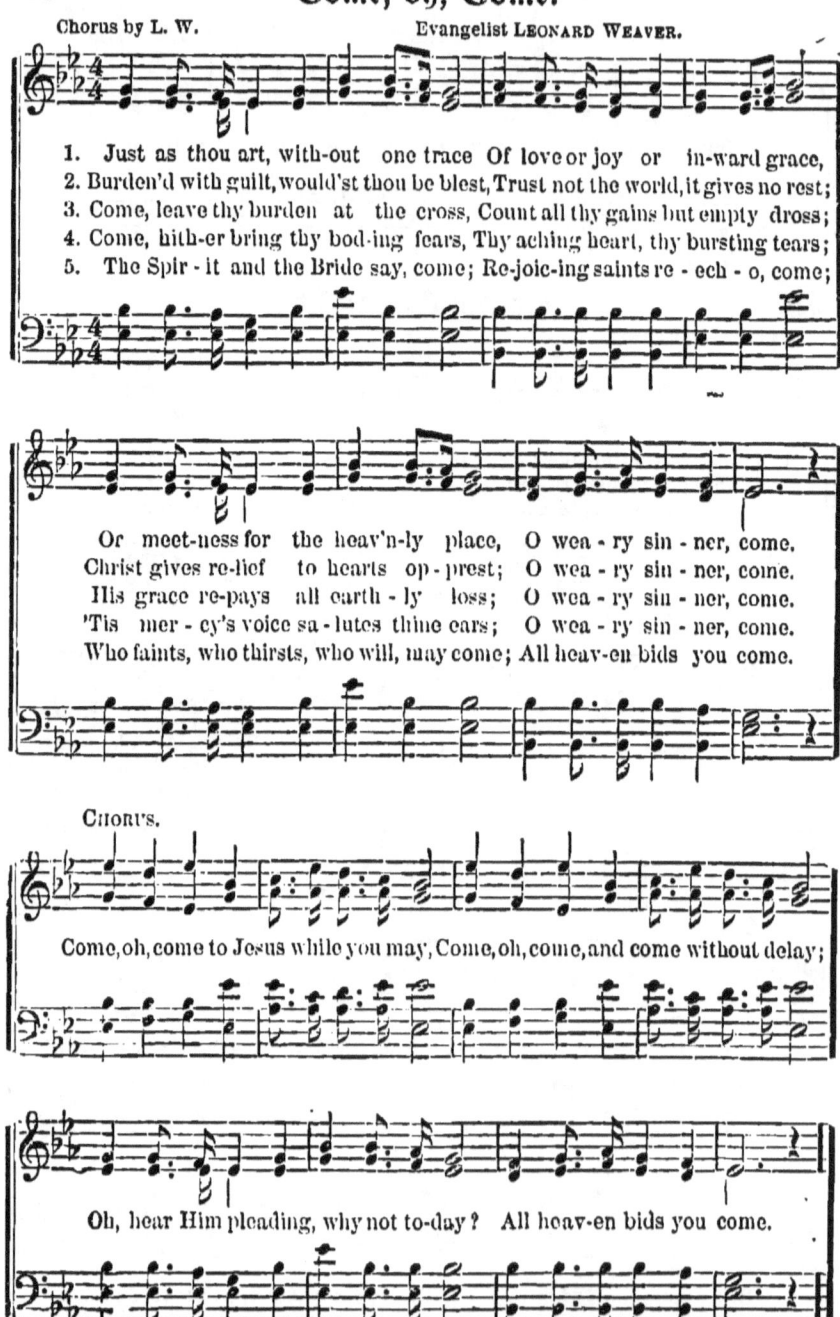

63. Bringing in the Sheaves.

"The harvest is the end of the world."—Matt. 13, 39.

Words from "Songs of Glory."   GEO. A. MINOR.

1. Sow-ing in the morn-ing, sow-ing seeds of kind-ness,
Sow-ing in the noon-tide and the dew-y eves; Waiting for the har-vest, and the time of reap-ing, We shall come re-joic-ing, bringing in the sheaves.

2. Sow-ing in the sun-shine, sow-ing in the shad-ows,
Fearing neither clouds nor winter's chilling breeze; By and by the har-vest, and the la-bor end-ed, We shall come re-joic-ing, bringing in the sheaves.

3. Go, then, ev-en weep-ing, sow-ing for the Mas-ter,
Tho' the loss sustain'd our spir-it oft-en grieves; When our weeping's o-ver, He will bid us wel-come, We shall come re-joic-ing, bringing in the sheaves.

CHORUS.
Bring-ing in the sheaves, Bring-ing in the sheaves,
Bring-ing in the sheaves, Bring-ing in the sheaves,
We shall come re-joic-ing, bringing in the sheaves,
We shall come re-joic - - (Omit) - - ing, bringing in the sheaves.

From "Gospel Echoes," by per.

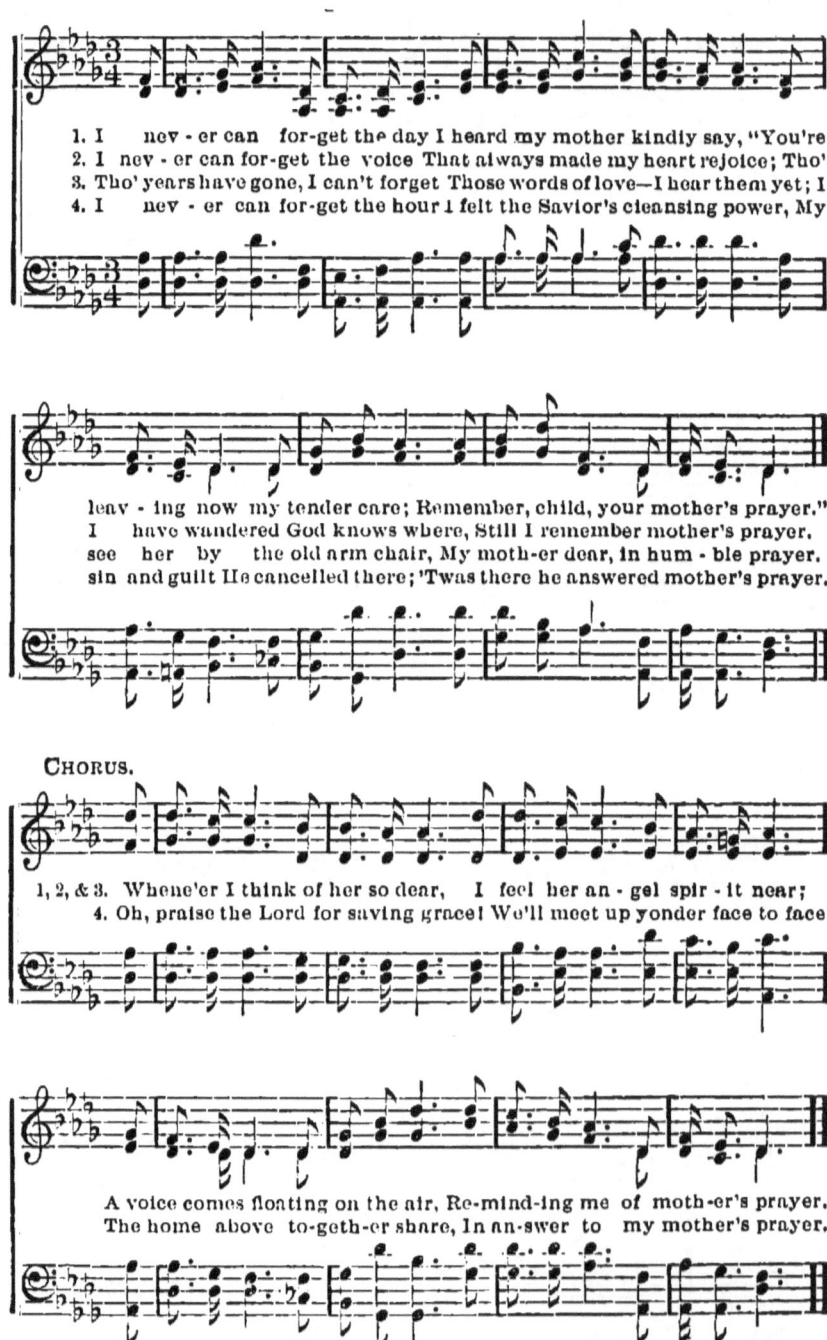

70. Leaning on the Everlasting Arms.

REV. E. A. HOFFMAN.   A. J. SHOWALTER.

1. What a fel-low-ship, what a joy divine, Lean-ing on the ev-er-
2. Oh, how sweet to walk in this pilgrim way, Lean-ing on the ev-er-
3. What have I to dread, what have I to fear, Lean-ing on the ev-er-

last-ing arms; What a bless-ed-ness, what a peace is mine,
last-ing arms; Oh, how bright the path grows from day to day,
last-ing arms? I have bless-ed peace with my Lord so near,

Lean-ing on the ev-er-last-ing arms.
Lean-ing on the ev-er-last-ing arms.
Lean-ing on the ev-er-last-ing arms.

REFRAIN.

Lean - - ing, lean - - ing, Safe and se-cure from all a-larms;
Lean-ing on Je-sus, Lean-ing on Je-sus,

Lean - - ing, lean - - ing, Lean-ing on the ev-er-last-ing arms.
Leaning on Jesus, leaning on Je-sus,

Copyright, by A. J. Showalter. By per.

5 Then, when on earth my work is past,
  And I have reached the goal,
  Oh, bear me to my home at last,
  An humble, grateful soul.
  Bear me home, bear me home,
  To my heav'nly home;
  Oh, bear me to my home at last,
  An humble, grateful soul.

6 A palm of victory I'll bear,
  Of vict'ry over sin;
  And I shall tell the angels there,
  How Jesus took me in.
  Tell them there, tell them there,
  Jesus took me in;
  Oh, I shall tell the angels there,
  How Jesus took me in.

From "Pearls of Paradise," by per.

75. Oh, What a Resting Place!

J. W. Van De Venter. W. S. Weeden.

1. I have found a friend divine, And his saving grace is mine; When I trusted in his word, Then I found the Lord. It is now so sweet to stay Where he wash'd my sins away, Where his Spirit fills my soul, Where he keeps me whole.
2. I will evermore abide Near the Saviour's wounded side—Always rest securely there, In his ten-der care. When the storms of life assail, When distress and grief prevail, He will fold me to his breast—Give me joy and rest.
3. Sinner, there is rest for thee At the cross of Calva-ry; Thy sal-vation is complete At the Saviour's feet. Come and rest beneath the cross; Count all else but earthly dross; Come, ye ruined by the fall, There is rest for all.

CHORUS.

{ Oh, what a resting place! Oh, what a-biding grace!
{ There was the blood applied, Now I am sat-is-fied;
{ Oh, what a rest-ing, a rest-ing place! Oh, what a-bid-ing, a-bid-ing grace!
{ There, oh, there was the blood ap-plied, Now, just now I am sat-is-fied;

Down at the cross of Jesus Where I found the blessed Saviour;
Oh, hal-le-lujah! praise his name forever- (*Omit.*) . . . . more.
Down at the cross, at the cross of Je-sus,
Oh, hal-le-lu-jah! I'll praise, I'll praise his

Copyright, 1895, by J. W. Van De Venter

77. Papa, Shall I Look For You?

Dedicated to the memory of AMY GRACE BEABLE.

For more than two years this child of Jesus, only nine years of age, had vainly besought her father to come to the Savior. Sickness at last seized her, and death came; but before the spirit took its flight she gave expression to these beautiful words, "I am going up; come, hurry up, mamma,—tell papa to come." Then, speaking to others, she said, "Won't *you* come?" Then, to her father, who had just arrived, she said, "Papa, come!" "I will come," said the father, "I can't have my child in heaven and not be there too."

Words and Music by J. W. VAN DE VENTER.

1. I am go-ing up, dear pa-pa, Are you coming by and by?
2. Won't you promise me, dear pa-pa? Je-sus wants you there, I know.
3. Yes, I'll come, my lit-tle darling, Calm your fears and doubt no more;
4. She has passed be-yond the riv-er, And we hear her voice no more;

Won't you come to see your darling In the home be-yond the sky?
Will you meet me up in heaven? Tell me now, be-fore I go.
I will meet my child in heaven, When this drea-ry life is o'er.
She is rest-ing, sweet-ly rest-ing, O-ver on the oth-er shore;

At the gate-way I'll be waiting When the lov-ing ones pass thro';
At the gate-way I'll be waiting When the lov-ing ones pass thro';
Tell the Sav-ior I am coming, That He saves your pa-pa, too;
But the Sav-ior is in-vit-ing, And the call is ev-er new:

I will see them as they en-ter; Pa-pa, shall I look for you?
I will see them as they en-ter; Pa-pa, shall I look for you?
Thro' His bless-ed love and mer-cy, By and by I'll be with you.
Will you hear the in-vi-ta-tion? Sinner, He is call-ing you!

Copyright, 1894, by J. W. Van De Venter.

Fall into Line, Boys.—Concluded.

79. Trusting Jesus.

"Trust in Him at all times."—*Ps. 62: 8.*

FAIRELIE THORNTON. JAMES WHARTON, Evangelist.

1. Sweet it is to trust in Jesus, When the way seems dark and long,
Sweet it is to trust in Jesus, When life's woes around us throng.
When the path we tread looks gloomy, And we nigh are lost again;
When we fix our eyes on Jesus, Oh, 'tis sweet to trust Him then.

2. Sweet it is to trust in Jesus, None like He our hearts can know,
Ev'ry secret of the spirit, Ev'ry depth of human woe
Jesus sees with clearer vision, Than can grasp a mortal's ken;
When we scarce can read the meaning, Oh, 'tis sweet to trust Him then.

3 Sweet it is to trust in Jesus,
  He can never prove untrue;
Earthly friends may any moment
  Change, and bid a cold adieu;
But our Savior will not leave us;
  Truer than the sons of men,
When they leave us, Christ is with us,
  Oh, 'tis sweet to trust Him then.

4 When our labors all seems useless,
  No one listens to our words;
When we strive in vain to waken
  In some heart the heavenly chords;
When we are by friends forsaken,
  Hated by our fellow men,
And we scarce can read the meaning,
  Oh, 'tis sweet to trust Him then.

Copyright, 1890, by Weeden & Wharton.

83. I Surrender All.
(DUET.)

J. W. Van DeVenter. W. S. Weeden.

1. All to Jesus I surrender, All to him I freely give;
   I will ever love and trust him, In his presence daily live.
2. All to Jesus I surrender, Humbly at his feet I bow,
   Worldly pleasures all forsaken, Take me, Jesus, take me now.
3. All to Jesus I surrender, Make me, Saviour, wholly thine;
   Let me feel the Holy Spirit, Truly know that thou art mine.

CHORUS.

I surrender all, I surrender all,
I surrender all. I surrender all,
All to thee, my blessed Saviour, I surrender all.

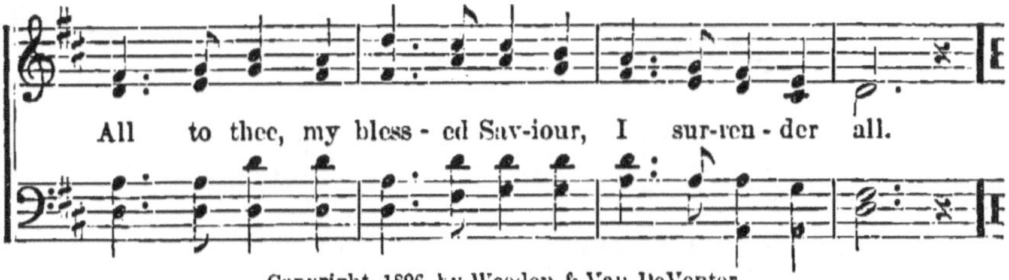

Copyright, 1896, by Weeden & Van DeVenter.

4. All to Jesus I surrender,
   Lord, I give myself to thee,
   Fill me with thy love and power,
   Let thy blessing fall on me.

5. All to Jesus I surrender,
   Now I feel the sacred flame;
   O the joy of full salvation!
   Glory, glory to his name!

He Saves Me.—Concluded.

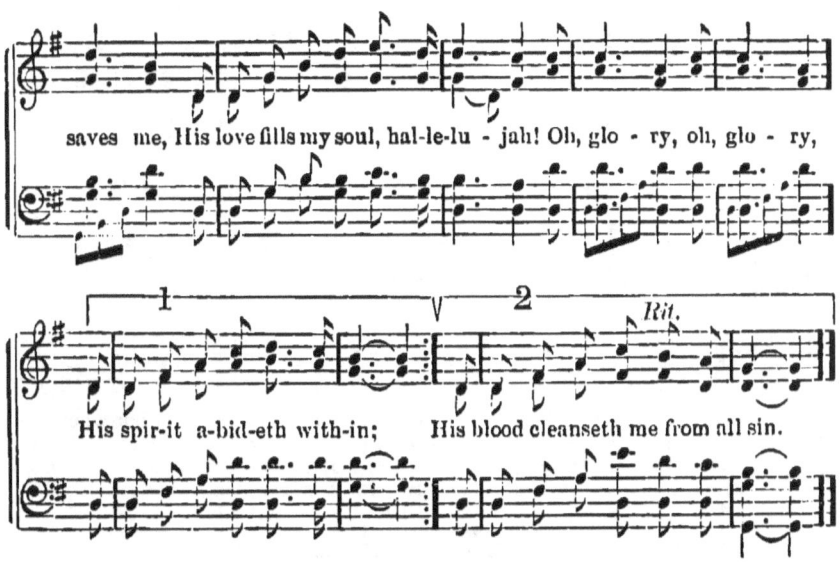

saves me, His love fills my soul, hal-le-lu - jah! Oh, glo - ry, oh, glo - ry, His spir-it a-bid-eth with-in; His blood cleanseth me from all sin.

85 Alas! and Did My Savior Bleed?
ISAAC WATTS.

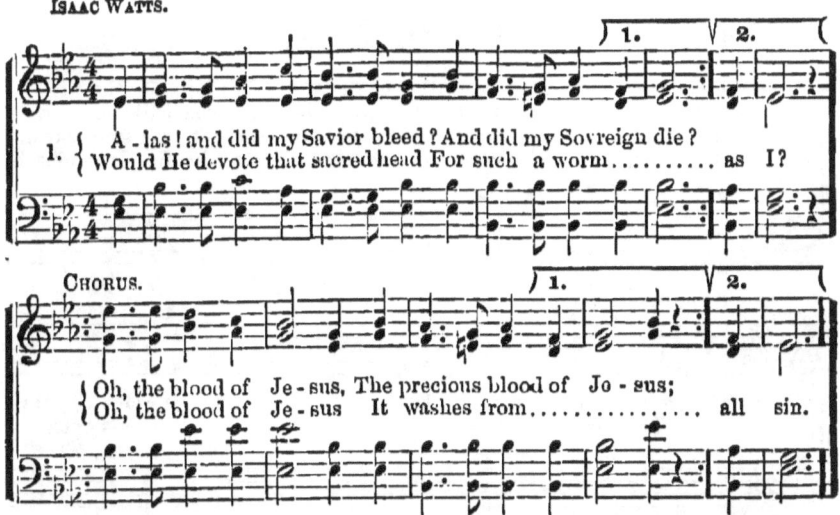

1. A - las! and did my Savior bleed? And did my Sovreign die?
Would He devote that sacred head For such a worm......... as I?

CHORUS.
Oh, the blood of Je - sus, The precious blood of Je - sus;
Oh, the blood of Je - sus It washes from............ all sin.

2 Was it for crimes that I have done,
  He groaned upon the tree?
  Amazing pity! grace unknown!
  And love beyond degree!

3 Well might the sun in darkness hide,
  And shut his glories in,
  When Christ, the mighty Maker, died,
  For man the creature's sin.

4 Thus might I hide my blushing face
  While His dear cross appears;
  Dissolve my heart in thankfulness,
  And melt mine eyes to tears.

5 But drops of grief can ne'er repay
  The debt of love I owe;
  Here, Lord, I give myself away,—
  'Tis all that I can do.

89. The Bridegroom Cometh!

Words and Melody by LEONARD WEAVER, Evangelist.

1. O brother, are you ready should the Bridegroom come? Are your lamps well trim'd and bright? For sure He will come, And the time will not be long; Are you read-y if He came to-night?
2. The trumpet will be sounded when the Bridegroom comes, And the grave yield up its prey, The dead shall a-rise And meet Him in the skies; Are you read-y for that glo-rious day?
3. It may be at the gloaming when the Bridegroom comes, Or the ris-ing of the sun, So we watch, work and pray, And go sing-ing on our way; To the faith-ful He will say "well done."

What a meeting it will be, When the Sav-ior we shall see, And as-cend-ing we shall meet Him in the sky; With Him we shall ev-er be, And from ev-'ry sin be free; Are you read-y for the midnight cry?
All the loved ones we shall meet, And with rapture we shall greet, All the ransom'd who have journey'd on be-fore; What a song of praise we'll sing When we stand around our King; Are you read-y for the heav'nly shore?
When the vic-to-ry is won We shall have a star-ry crown, And in wor-ship we shall cast it at His feet, Cry-ing, "Worthy is the Lamb To receive the song and psalm; Are you read-y for that bliss complete?

CHORUS.

Yes, I am ready, yes, I am ready, ready, ready,

1. Read-y for my Lord to come!
2. Read-y for the call, Come home!

Yes, I'm ready, O,

Copyright, 1895, by Leonard Weaver.

3 Sweet fields beyond the swelling flood,
  Stand dressed in living green;
  So to the Jew old Canaan stood,
  While Jordan rolled between.

4 Could we but climb where Moses stood,
  And view the landscape o'er;
  Not Jordan's stream, nor death's cold flood
  Should fright us from the shore.

Copyright, 1895, by W. C. Weeden.

94. The Blood of Jesus Cleanseth Me.

The Blood of Jesus Christ cleanseth us from all sin. 1 John 1: 7.

Rev. W. H. Sheak. Chas. H. Gabriel.

1. O, the blood of Jesus cleanseth me from all my sin! Praise his holy name so precious, I am pure with-in! Tho' my sins were scarlet, they are whit-er now than snow; Once my soul was red with crimson, now 'tis clean I know.
2. I'm so happy now in Jesus, and I know he's mine: He's the tender Shepherd of my soul—my guide di-vine, E'er he leads me by the wa-ters that are still and cool, Thro' the pastures ev-er green, be-side the sha-dy pool.
3. Let thy blood, O precious Saviour, always be applied To my falt'ring heart, and dai-ly life, whate'er be-tide; Till my life be-low is end-ed, and my work is done, And I stand with thee triumphant, and a crown have won.

CHORUS.

Praise the name of Jesus, for His blood it cleanseth me! All the chains of sin are broken, now my soul is free! O, the blood, the precious blood, it

Copyright, 1896, by R. C. Ward. By per.

The Blood of Jesus Cleanseth Me.—CONCLUDED.

makes me white as snow! All my life and all my sins are underneath its flow.

95. Lord, I'm Coming Home.

W. J. K.
With great feeling.
W. J. KIRKPATRICK. By per.

1. I've wandered far a-way from God, Now I'm com-ing home;
2. I've wast-ed ma-ny pre-cious years, Now I'm com-ing home;
3. I'm tired of sin and stray-ing, Lord, Now I'm com-ing home;
4. My soul is sick, my heart is sore, Now I'm com-ing home;

FINE.

The paths of sin too long I've trod, Lord, I'm com-ing home.
I now re-pent with bit-ter tears, Lord, I'm com-ing home.
I'll trust thy love, be-lieve thy word, Lord, I'm com-ing home.
My strength re-new, my hope re-store, Lord, I'm com-ing home.

D. S.—O-pen wide thine arms of love, Lord, I'm com-ing home.

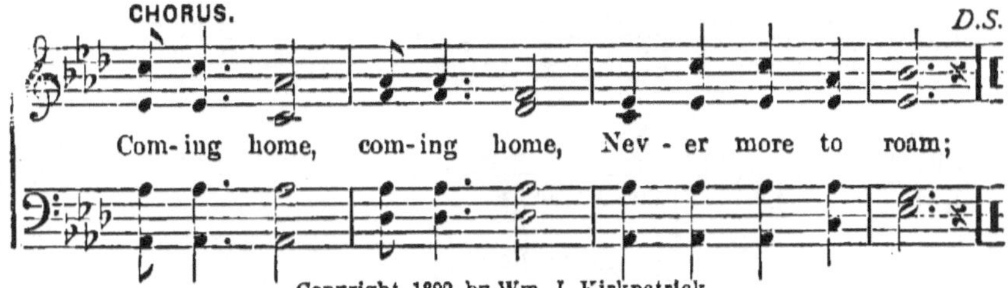

CHORUS.
D.S.

Com-ing home, com-ing home, Nev-er more to roam;

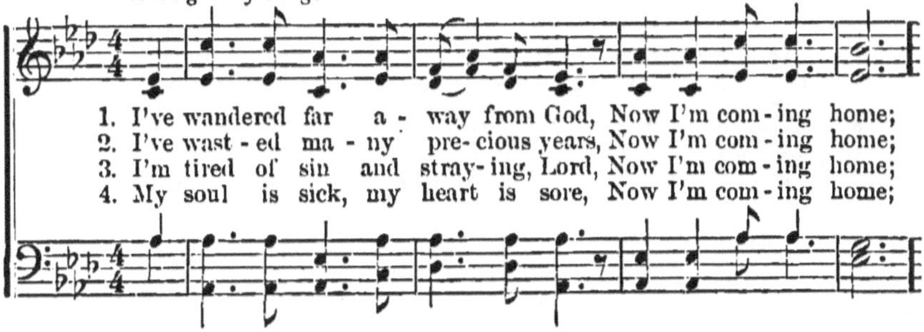

Copyright, 1892, by Wm. J. Kirkpatrick.

5 My only hope, my only plea,
   Now I'm coming home,
That Jesus died, and died for me,
   Lord, I'm coming home.

6 I need his cleansing blood I know,
   Now I'm coming home;
O, wash me whiter than the snow,
   Lord, I'm coming home.

3 I'll praise Him while He gives me breath,
   Love found me;
For saving from an endless death,
   Love found me;
Christ is my advocate above,
   Love found me;
I'm yoked to Him in perfect love,
   Love found me.

4 And when I reach the gold-paved street,
   Love found me;
I'll sit adoring at His feet,
   Love found me;
And sing hosannas round the throne,
   Love found me;
Where I shall know as I am known,
   Love found me.

Copyright, 1890, by H. L. Gilmour. By per.

I will Work for Jesus.—Concluded.

99. Cleansing Wave.

PHŒBE PALMER.   Mrs. J. F. KNAPP.

CHORUS.

1 Oh, now I see the cleansing wave!
  The fountain deep and wide;
Jesus, my Lord, mighty to save,
  Points to His wounded side.

Cho.—The cleansing stream, I see, I see;
  I plunge, and oh, it cleanseth me!
Oh, praise the Lord! it cleanseth me!
  It cleanseth me—yes, cleanseth me.
By permission.

2 I rise to walk in heaven's own light,
  Above the world of sin, [white,
With heart made pure and garments
  And Christ enthroned within.

3 Amazing grace! 'tis heaven below
  To feel the blood applied;
And Jesus, only Jesus, know,
  My Jesus crucified.

We are Soldiers.—Concluded.

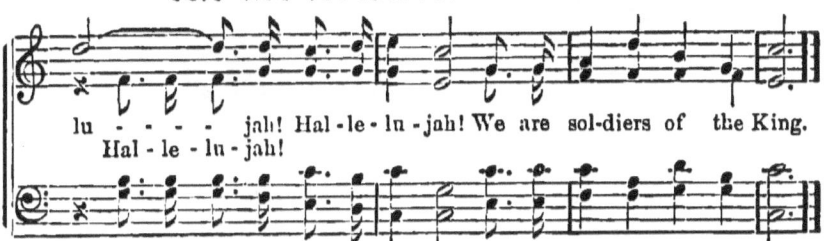

lu — — — jah! Hal-le-lu-jah! We are sol-diers of the King.
Hal-le-lu-jah!

101. Invitation Hymn.

1 Come, ye sinners, poor and needy,
Weak and wounded, sick and sore;
Jesus ready stands to save you,
Full of pity, love, and power:
He is able,
He is willing: doubt no more.

2 Now, ye needy, come and welcome;
God's free bounty glorify;
True belief and true repentance,
Every grace that brings you nigh,
Without money,
Come to Jesus Christ and buy.

3 Let not conscience make you linger,
Nor of fitness fondly dream;
All the fitness He requireth
Is to feel your need of Him:
This He gives you;
'Tis the Spirit's glimmering beam.

4 Come, ye weary, heavy-laden,
Bruised and mangled by the fall;

If you tarry till you're better,
You will never come at all;
Not the righteous,—
Sinners, Jesus came to call.

5 Agonizing in the garden,
Your Redeemer prostrate lies;
On the bloody tree behold Him!
Hear Him cry before He dies,
"It is finished!"
Sinners, will not this suffice?

6 Lo! the incarnate God, ascending,
Pleads the merit of His blood:
Venture on Him, venture freely;
Let no other trust intrude;
None but Jesus
Can do helpless sinners good.

7 Saints and angels, joined in concert,
Sing the praises of the Lamb;
While the blissful seats of heaven
Sweetly echo with His name:
Hallelujah!
Sinners here may do the same.
JOSEPH HART.

Come, Ye Sinners.
JEREMIAH INGALLS.

1. { Come, ye sin-ners, poor and need-y, Weak and wounded, sick and sore; }
   { Je-sus read-y stands to save you, Full of pit-y, love, and pow'r. }
D.C.—Glo-ry, hon-or, and sal-va-tion! Christ the Lord is come to reign.

CHORUS.
Turn to the Lord, and seek sal-va-tion, Sound the praise of His dear name;

107. Shall We Gather at the River?

R. L.   Rev. R. Lowry. By per.

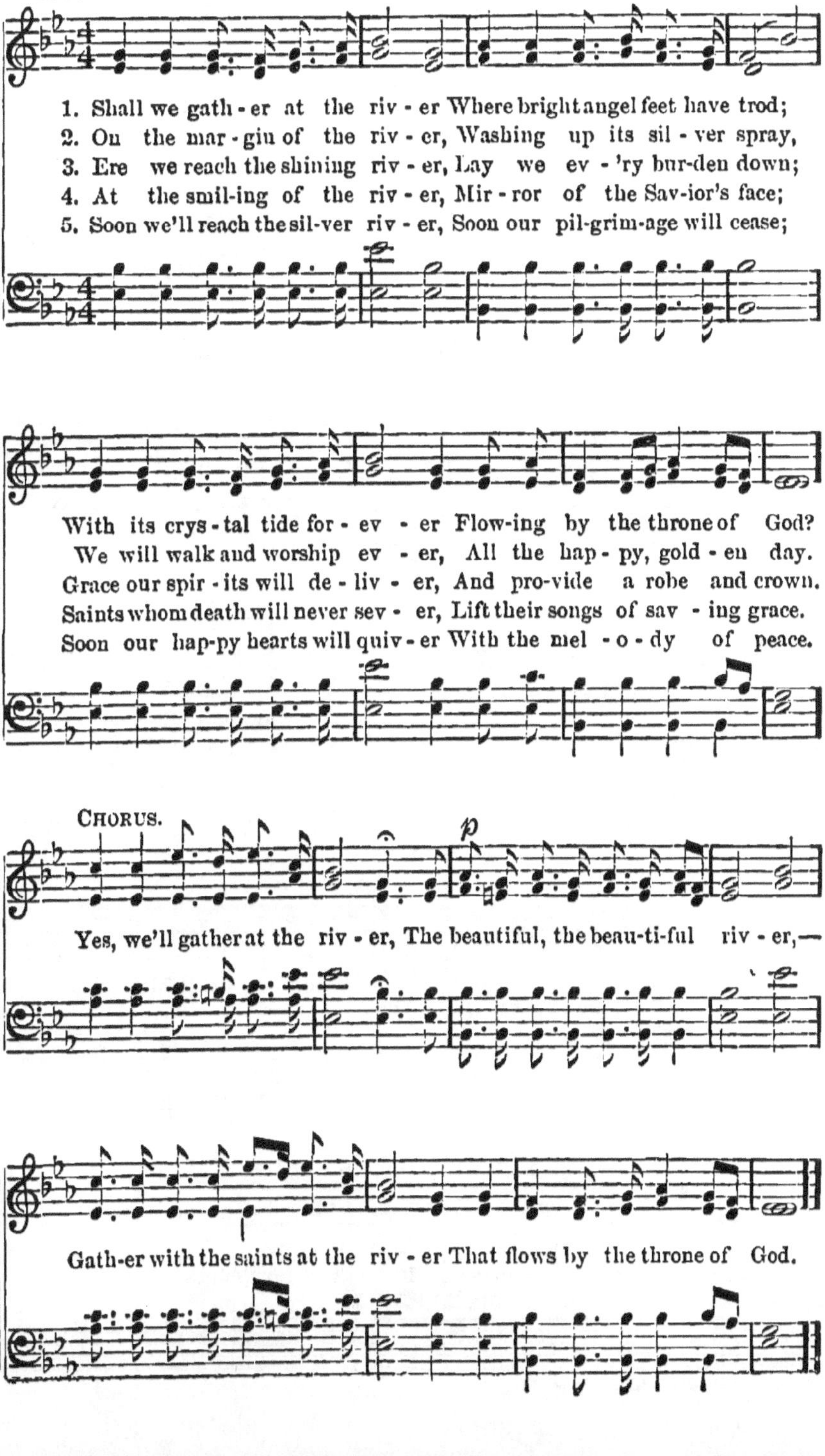

1. Shall we gath-er at the riv-er Where bright angel feet have trod;
2. On the mar-gin of the riv-er, Washing up its sil-ver spray,
3. Ere we reach the shining riv-er, Lay we ev-'ry bur-den down;
4. At the smil-ing of the riv-er, Mir-ror of the Sav-ior's face;
5. Soon we'll reach the sil-ver riv-er, Soon our pil-grim-age will cease;

With its crys-tal tide for-ev-er Flow-ing by the throne of God?
We will walk and worship ev-er, All the hap-py, gold-en day.
Grace our spir-its will de-liv-er, And pro-vide a robe and crown.
Saints whom death will never sev-er, Lift their songs of sav-ing grace.
Soon our hap-py hearts will quiv-er With the mel-o-dy of peace.

CHORUS.

Yes, we'll gather at the riv-er, The beautiful, the beau-ti-ful riv-er,—

Gath-er with the saints at the riv-er That flows by the throne of God.

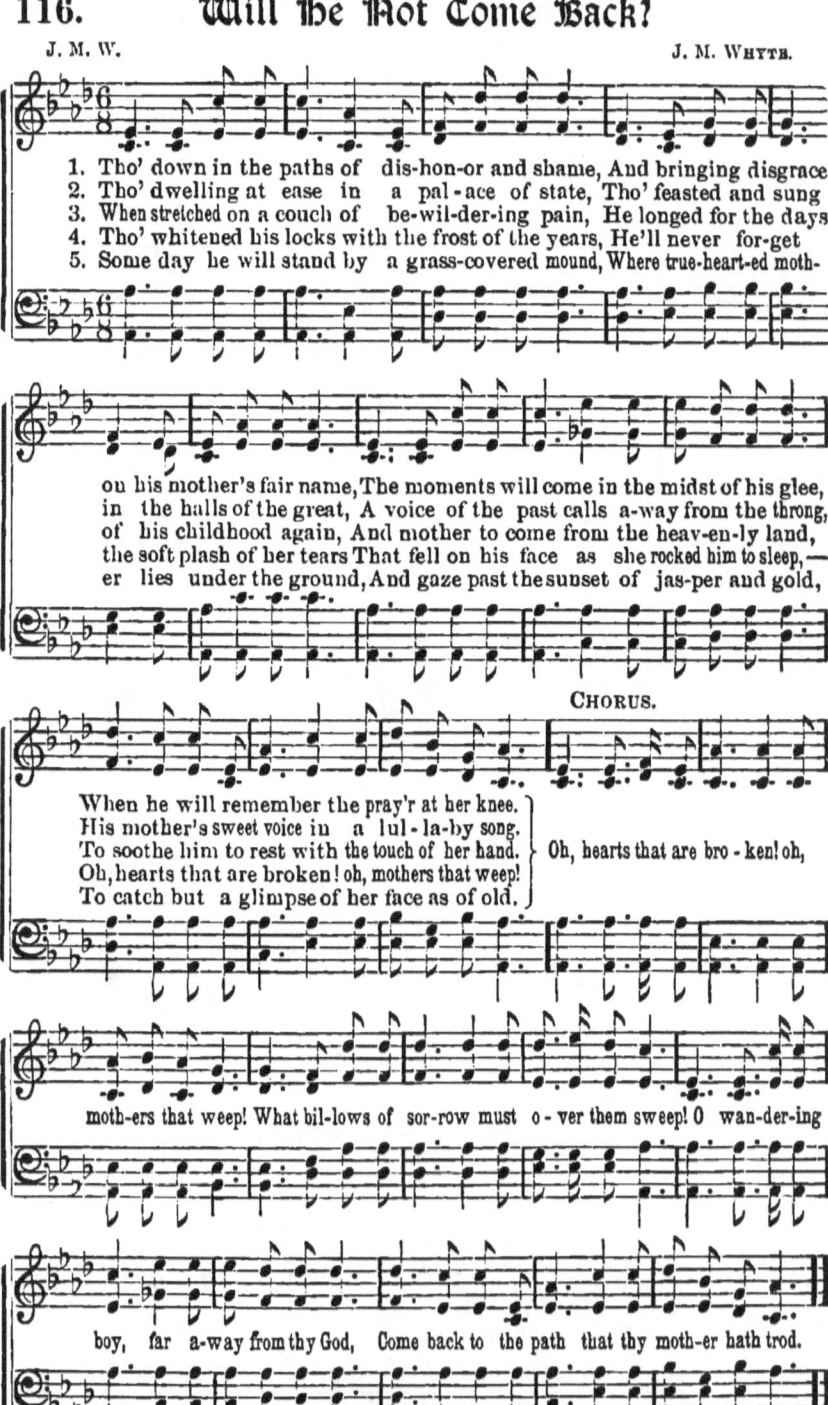

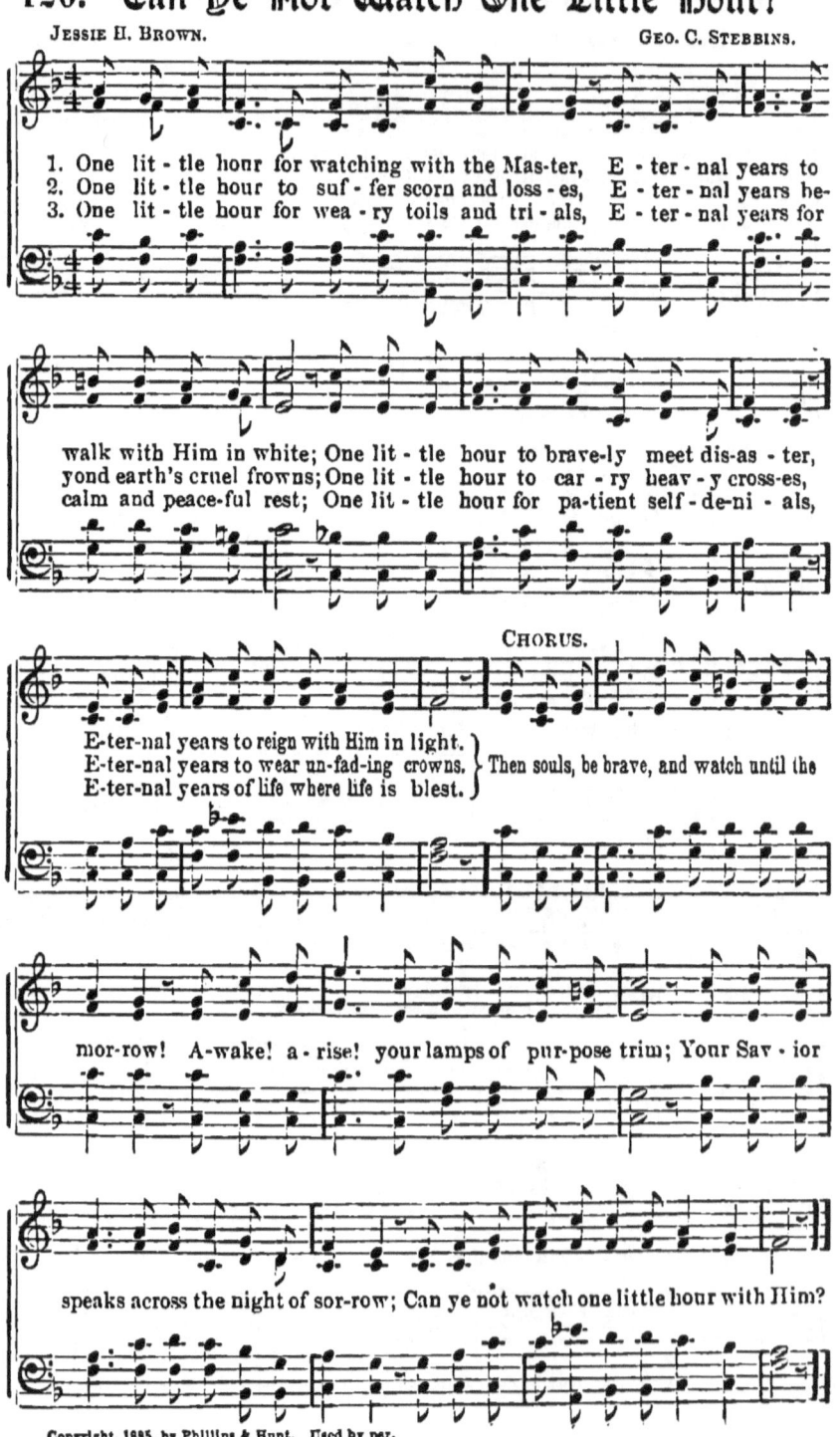

121. The Call for Reapers.

J. O. THOMPSON.
J. B. O. CLEMM.

Spirited.

1. Far and near the fields are teem-ing With the waves of rip-ened grain; Far and near their gold is gleam-ing O'er the sun-ny slope and plain.
2. Send them forth with morn's first beam-ing, Send them in the noon-tide's glare; When the sun's last rays are gleam-ing, Bid them gath-er ev-'ry-where.
3. O thou, whom thy Lord is send-ing, Gath-er now the sheaves of gold, Heav'nward then at ev-'ning wend-ing Thou shalt come with joy un-told.

CHORUS.

Lord of har-vest, send forth reap-ers! Hear us, Lord, to Thee we cry; Send them now the sheaves to gath-er, Ere the har-vest time pass by.

Used by per. Hunt & Eaton, owners of Copyright.

Sunlight all the Way. Concluded.

with my Sav-ior near, There is bright and blessed sunlight all the way,

123. Face the Other Way.

E. R. LATTA.   FRANK M. DAVIS.

1. Broad the road of e-vil, And the crowd is there, Sowing to the whirlwind,
2. What the Lord commandeth, Hear it and o-bey, Ere too late for-ev-er,
3. In the way so nar-row, Where His people go, Let your feet be treading,
4. "Blessed of my Fa-ther!" Hear the Savior say; E'en this moment choose Him,

Lay-ing up de-spair; If you're in the broad road, Flee from it to-day,
Face the oth-er way; If you're in the broad road, Flee from it to-day,
Sin-ner here be-low; If you're in the broad road, Flee from it to-day,
Face the oth-er way; If you're in the broad road, Flee from it to-day,

D. S.—*If you're in the broad road, Flee from it to-day,*

FINE. CHORUS.

If you're looking sinwards, Face the oth-er way. Face the oth-er way,
If you're looking sinwards, Face the oth-er way.

D. S.

Face the oth-er way, If you're looking sinwards, Face the oth-er way.

Copyright, 1893, by H. H. Hadley.

Seeking the Lost—Concluded.

Jesus, the Lamb for sin-ners slain, for sin-ners slain.

Jesus, the Lamb............ for sin - ners slain...............

125 Jesus is Mine.

Mrs. C. J. Bonar.   T. E. Perkins.

1. Fade, fade, each earth-ly joy, Je-sus is mine! Break, ev-'ry
2. Fare-well, ye dreams of night, Je-sus is mine! Lost in this
3. Fare-well, mor-tal-i-ty Je-sus is mine! Wel-come, e-

ten-der tie, Je-sus is mine! Dark is the wil-der-ness,
dawning light, Je-sus is mine! All that my soul has tried
ter-ni-ty, Je-sus is mine! Wel-come, O loved and blest,

Earth has no rest-ing-place, Je-sus a-lone can bless, Je-sus is mine!
Left but a dis-mal void, Je-sus has sat-is-fied, Je-sus is mine!
Welcome, sweet scenes of rest, Welcome, my Savior's breast, Je-sus is mine!

Used by permission.

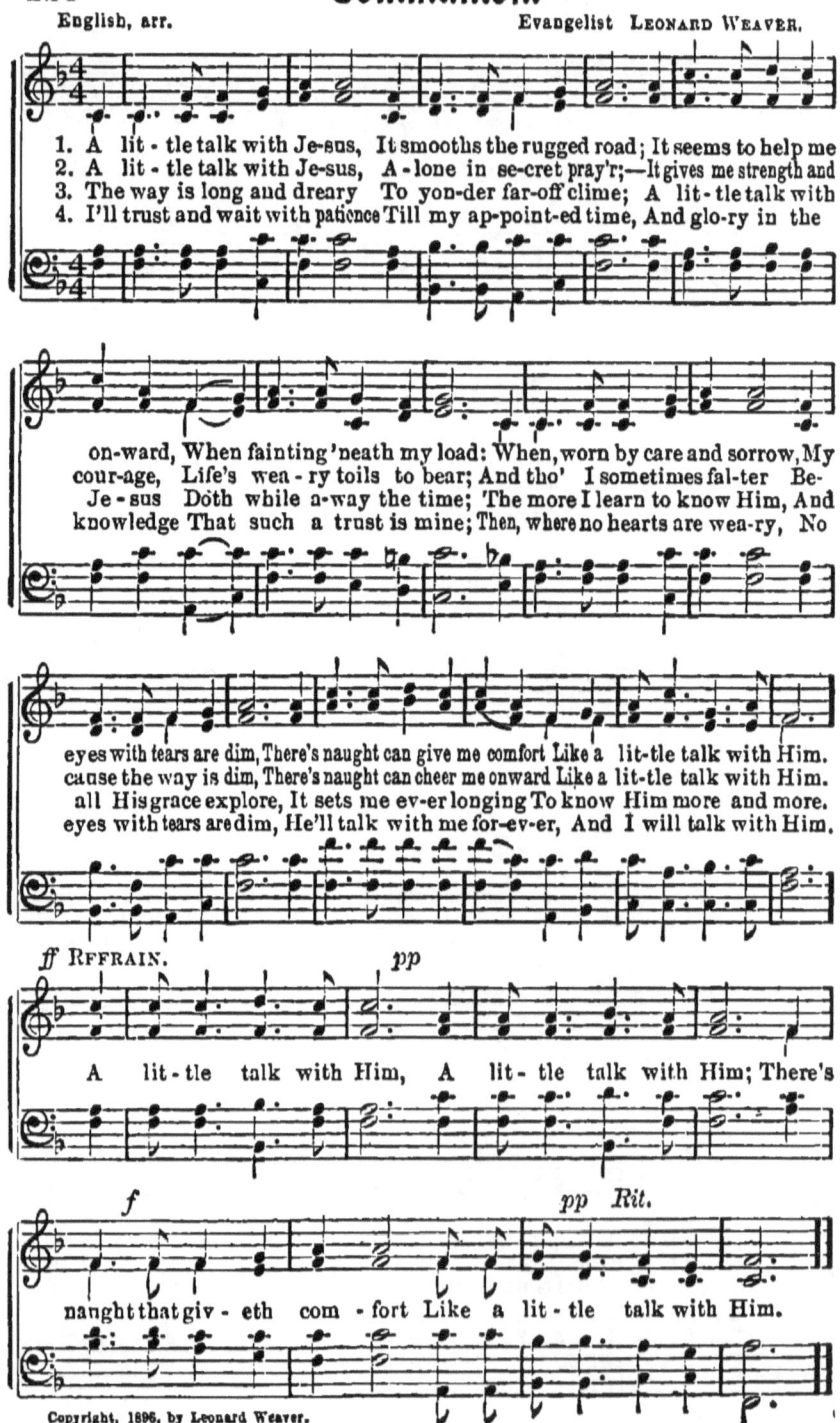

130. Come to the Savior.

"And him that cometh to me I will in no wise cast out."—John 6: 37.

Rev. Elisha A. Hoffman.   A. F. Myers.

Moderato.

1. Je - sus is call-ing, call-ing for thee, Hear-est thou not His im-por-tunate plea? Oh, by the spear-wound pierced in His side, Haste to be saved by the Cru-ci-fied.
2. Je - sus is pleading, pleading with thee, Was ev-er mer-cy so rich and so free? Won-der-ful grace He waits to be-stow, Is it not strange He should love thee so?
3. Je - sus is wait-ing, wait-ing for thee, Love could not pur-er and ho - li - er be, Oh, for the blood poured out for thy soul, Come to this Sav-ior and be made whole.
4. Je - sus is here, but soon He may go, Shall He bear with Him thy sins and thy woe? Oh, then, en-treat Him, ere He de-part, Free-ly to par-don and cleanse thy heart.

CHORUS.

1st. Come to the Savior, no long-er de-lay, Trust in His love and ac-cept Him to-day; Ten-der-ly, lov-ing-ly calls He to thee, List to His pleading, be-lieve and be free.

2d. Wonderful grace! how it sat-is-fies me, Won-der-ful mer-cy! so rich and so free; Would you a child of the cov - e - nant be? Je - sus can save you—He sweet-ly saved me.

From "The Searchlight." By per.

135. Oh, It is Wonderful.

E. C. GREEN. Rewritten.   Rev. ELISHA A. HOFFMAN.

1. Can it be that Jesus bought me, And on the hallowed cross atoned for me,
2. Praise His name, He sought and found me, Saved me from wandering and brought me near;
3. It was months He had been waiting, Waiting the dawning of the precious hour;
4. From that hour He has been seeking, How He may fill me with His precious love;

Loved me, chose me ere I knew Him? Oh, what a precious, precious Friend is He?
Free - ly now His grace bestowing, Jesus is growing unto me more dear.
When I should at last be yielding, Yielding to Jesus ev'ry ransomed pow'r.
How He may thro' grace transform me, Meet for the fellowship of saints above.

CHORUS.

Oh, it is won-der-ful, ve-ry, ve-ry won-der-ful,

1. All His grace so rich and free!
[Omit. . . . .] All His love and grace to me!

5 As I think of all, I marvel
   Why in such patience He my good
     has sought,
   And bestowed His grace upon me,
   And in my spirit such a change
     has wrought.

6 So I cry, with love o'erflowing:
   "Unto the Savior be eternal
     praise,"
   Who redeemed me, soul and body,
   Filling with gladness all my
     earthly days.

Copyright, 1891, by THE HOFFMAN MUSIC CO.,

137. The Savior's Love.

Mrs. Katharine E. Purvis. W. S. Weeden.

1. How precious the love of my Sav-ior, Since first I believed on His name,
2. How ten-der the love of my Sav-ior! I sought Him when grieved and oppressed,
3. How changeless the love of my Sav-ior! Tho' flesh and heart fail, He will prove
4. How might-y the love of my Sav-ior! He broke the strong bars of the tomb;

When la-den with guilt and with sor-row To Cal-va-ry's foun-tain I came.
He lift-ed my bur-dens and gave me A fore-taste of heav-en-ly rest.
My strength and my por-tion for-ev-er, In man-sions of glo-ry a-bove.
No e-vil I fear since my Shepherd Has robbed the dark valley of gloom.

CHORUS.

His love, ev-'ry oth-er ex-cell-ing, So rich, so exhaustless, and free,

Ac-cept-ed my heart as its dwelling, And now is a-bid-ing with me.

Copyright, 1896, by W. S. Weeden.

139. Nearer the Cross.

"The cross of our Lord Jesus Christ."—GAL. 6: 14.

F. J. CROSBY. Mrs. J. F. KNAPP.

1. "Near-er the cross!" my heart can say, I am com-ing near-er; Near-er the cross from day to day, I am com-ing near-er; Near-er the cross where Je-sus died, Near-er the fountain's crimson tide, Near-er my Sav-ior's wound-ed side, I am com-ing near-er, I am com-ing near-er.

2. Near-er the Christian's mer-cy-seat, I am com-ing near-er; Feasting my soul on man-na sweet, I am com-ing near-er; Stronger in faith, more clear I see Je-sus who gave Himself for me; Near-er to Him I still would be: Still I'm com-ing near-er, Still I'm com-ing near-er.

3. Near-er in pray'r my hope aspires, I am com-ing near-er; Deep-er the love my soul de-sires, I am com-ing near-er; Near-er the end of toil and care, Near-er the joy I long to share, Near-er the crown I soon shall wear: I am com-ing near-er, I am com-ing near-er.

Used by per.

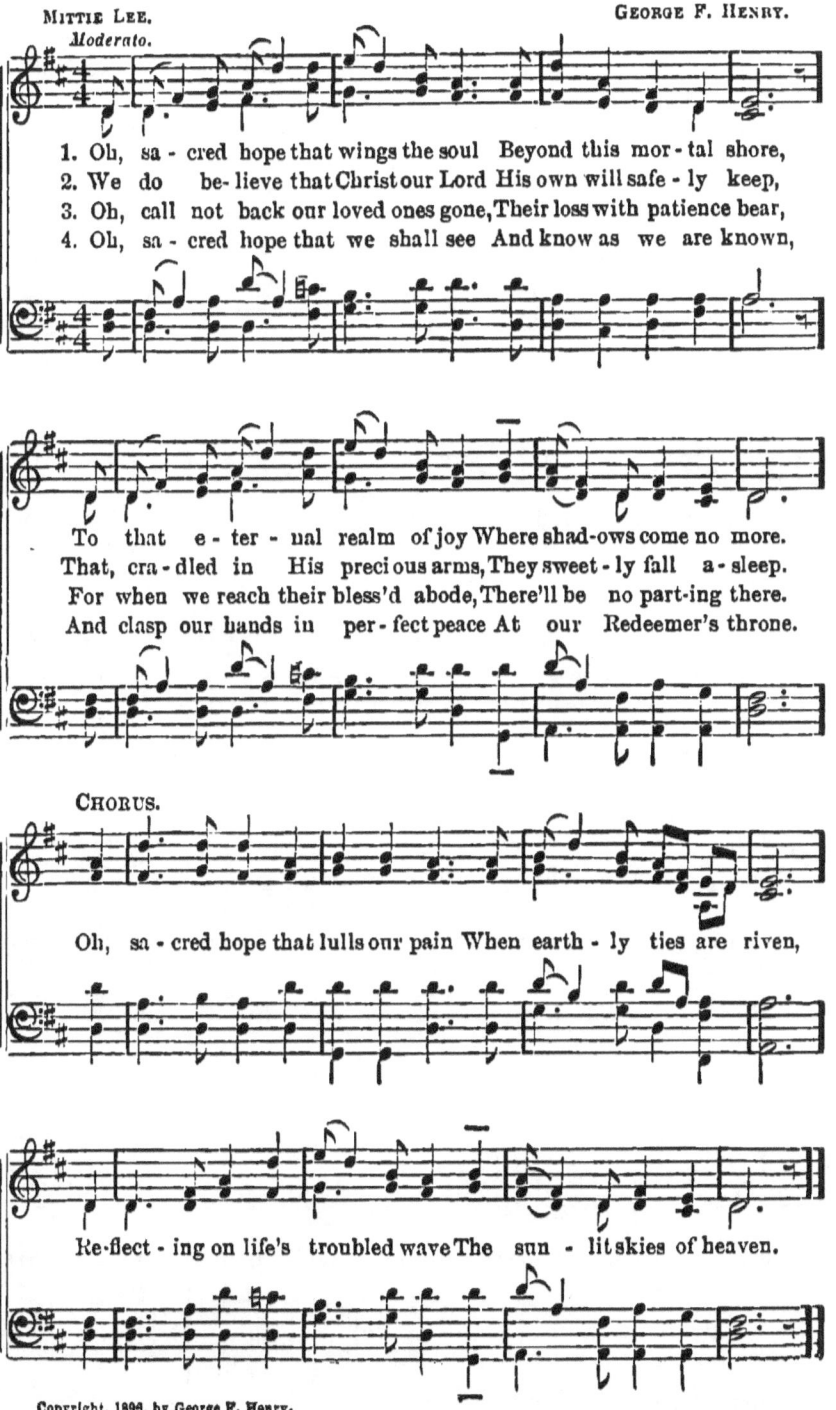

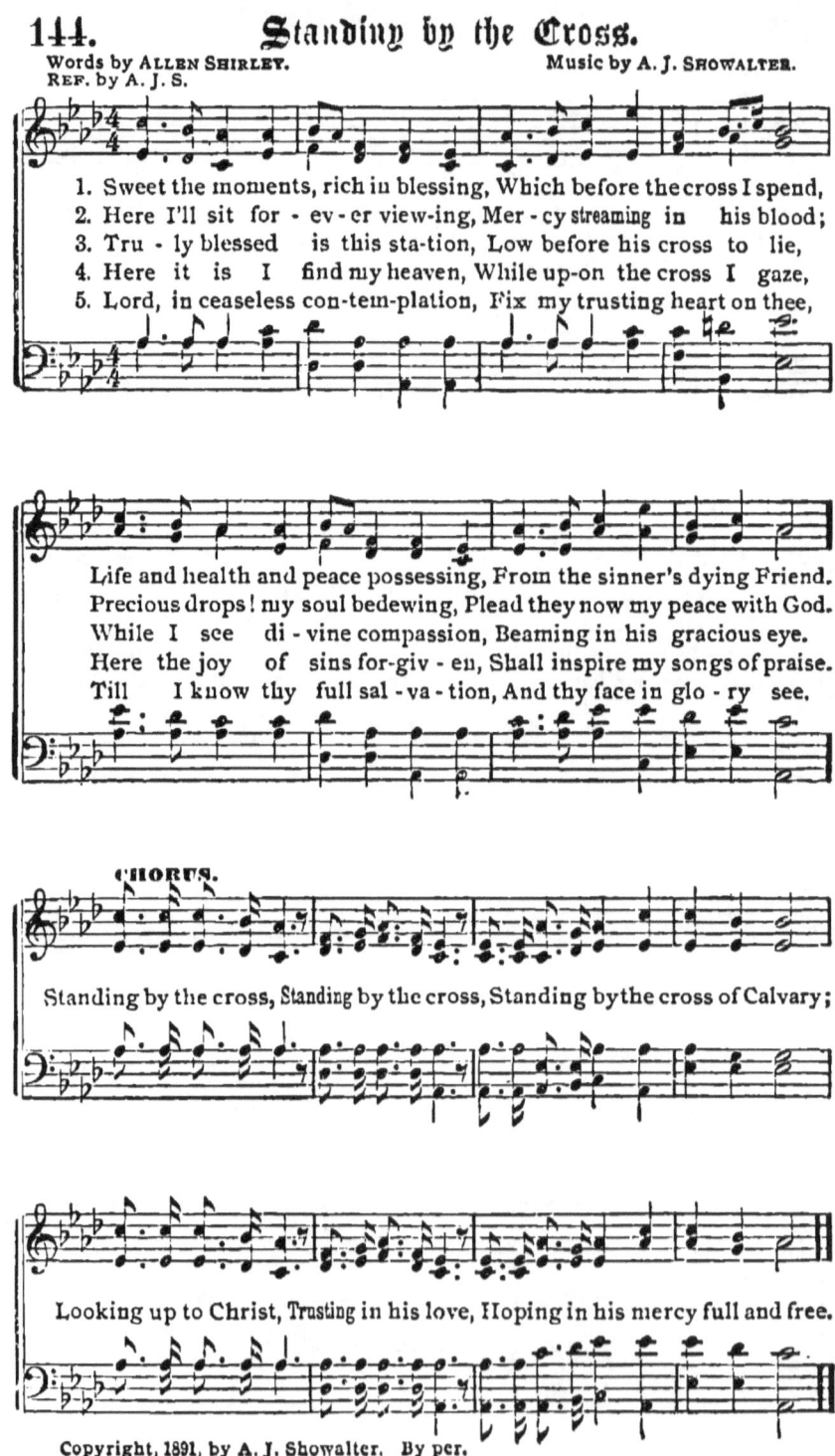

145. All the Way to Calvary.

Mrs. W. G. MOYER & I. H. M.   I. H. MEREDITH. Cho. arr.

1. Oh, how dark the night that wrapt my spir-it round! Oh, how deep the woe my Sav-ior found When He walked a-cross the wa-ters of my soul, Bade my night dis-perse and made me whole.
2. Tremblingly a sin-ner bowed be-fore his face, Naught I knew of par-don, God's free grace, Heard a voice so melt-ing, "Cease thy wild re-gret, Je-sus bought thy par-don, paid thy debt."
3. Oh, 'twas wondrous love the Sav-ior show'd for me, When He left His throne for Cal-va-ry, When He trod the wine-press, trod it all a-lone, Praise His name for-ev-er, make it known.

CHORUS.

All the way to Cal-va-ry He went for me, He went for me, He went for me, All the way to Cal-va-ry He went for me, He died to set me free.

Copyright, 1894, by I. H. Meredith.

146. Tell it Out!

FRANCES R. HAVERGAL.   W. S. WEEDEN.

1. Tell it out a-mong the na-tions that the Lord is King; Tell it out! Tell it out! Tell it out among the nations, bid them shout and sing; Tell it out! . . . Tell it out! Tell it out with ad-o-ration that He shall increase, That the mighty King of glory is the King of peace; Tell it

2. Tell it out a-mong the peo-ple that the Sav-ior reigns; Tell it out! Tell it out! Tell it out among the heathen, bid them break their chains; Tell it out! . . . Tell it out! Tell it out among the weeping ones that Je-sus lives, Tell it out among the weary ones what rest He gives, Tell it

3. Tell it out a-mong the peo-ple, Je-sus reigns a-bove; Tell it out! Tell it out! Tell it out among the nations that His reign is love; Tell it out! . . . Tell it out! Tell it out among the high-ways and the lanes at home, Let it ring across the mountains and the ocean's foam, That the

tell it out!

Copyright, 1896, by W. S. WEEDEN.

Tell it Out!

147. Shall my Lamp be Empty.

E. R. LATTA. H. N. LINCOLN.

With varied expression.

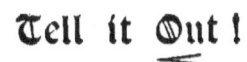

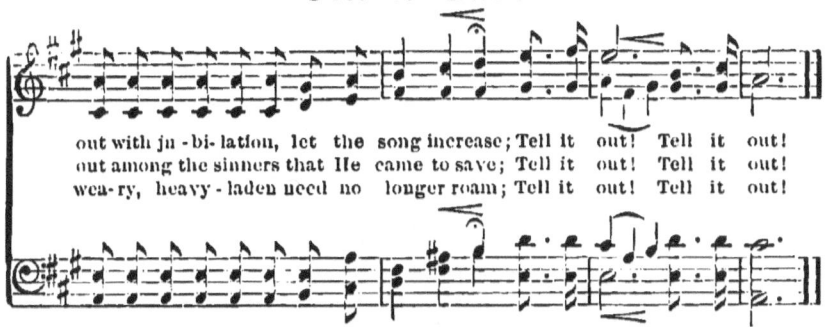

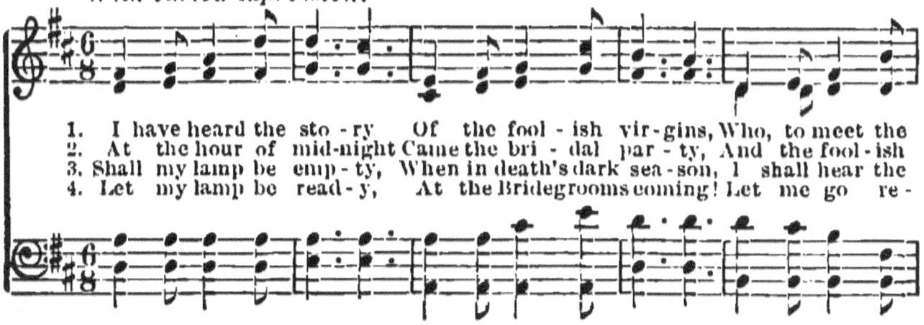

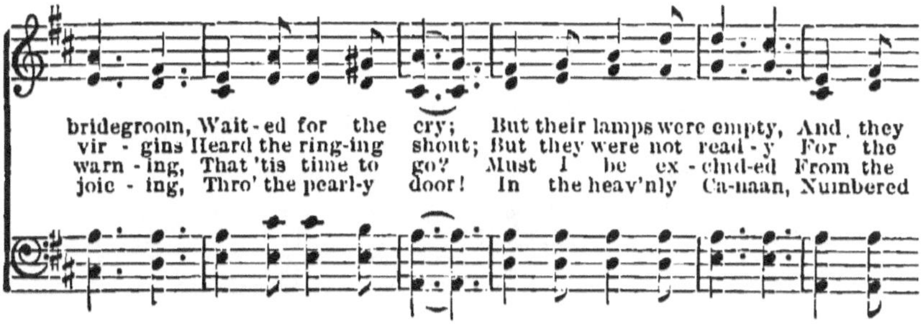

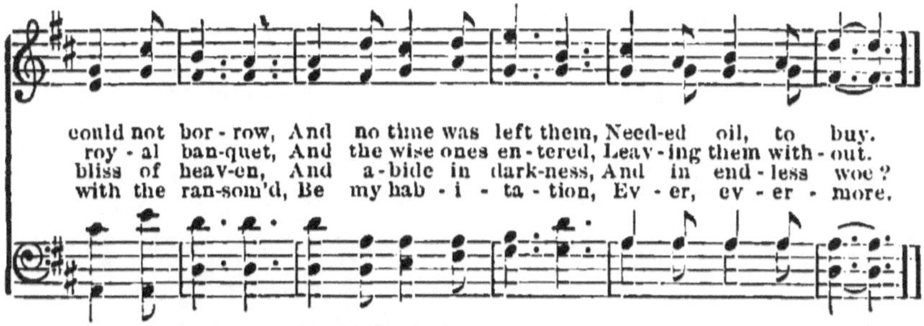

149. He is Calling,—Will You Come.

Mrs. Frank A. Breck.   Frank M. Davis.
By Per.

1. There is One who long hath sought you, Who would bless your needy soul, Great salvation he hath brought you, Freely he will make you whole.
2. There is One with love undying, Who himself for sinners gave, And upon that love relying, You shall find him strong to save.
3. Oh! the depths of love unsounded, It can reach the deepest woe, Will you take that love unbounded, All its blessedness to know.
4. Jesus calls you, hear and heed him, From his love turn not away, He is calling, O you need him, Come to Jesus, come to-day.

CHORUS.
He is calling, will you come, will you come, He is calling, will you come, will you come, Jesus loves you, he will save you, He is calling, will you come.

Copyright, 1896, by Frank M. Davis.

Hark, Hark! My Soul!—CONCLUDED.

152. The Welcome Home.

J. W. Van De Venter.   M. Lindsay.

1. As we watch the sails ap-pear-ing, Scan the wide ex-tend-ed main,
2. It is bless-ed to re-member, Those we love though far a-way,
3. Sweet the years but short-ly o-ver, Life is chang-ing day by day,

Look-ing for the dear ones com-ing, Hop-ing soon to meet a-gain,
And we long to see the morning, Of the glad re-un-ion day,
Mor-tals come and go like flow-ers, Live to bloom, then fade a-way,

It reminds us of the greet-ing, Waiting us be-yond the sky,
So we think of those in heav-en, Watching as the moments fly,
But our dear ones o-ver yon-der, Nev-er leave us, nev-er die.

When we gath-er at the riv-er, By and by, By and by;
Wait-ing for the fi-nal meet-ing, By and by, By and by;
We shall strike glad hands for-ev-er, By and by, By and by;

When we gath-er at the riv-er, By and by, By and by.
Wait-ing for the fi-nal meet-ing, By and by, By and by.
We shall strike glad hands for-ev-er, By and by, By and by.

Copyright, 1896, by WEEDEN & VAN DE VENTER.

153. The Morning Cometh!

LEONARD WEAVER, Evangelist. W. S. WEEDEN.

1. Lift up your heads, ye pilgrims, And view yon eastern sky, The night of sin is ending, The morning draweth nigh. The day foretold by prophets Will soon be ushered in, When Christ, the one who suffered, The world shall own as King.

2. Lift up your heads, ye pilgrims, And watch the morning break, For lo, Christ's glorious coming The thrones of earth will shake, See those who do not own Him In mountains seek to hide, Whilst those who love and trust Him Still in His grace confide.

3. Lift up your heads, ye pilgrims, For 'tis the Bridegroom comes With trumpet voice to call you Forth to His royal throne, See that your lamps are burning, Your garments pure and white, That He may find you watching And walking in the light.

4. Lift up your heads, ye pilgrims, Sing in that gladsome day, Nought but the Savior's coming The tide of sin can stay, Creation groans whilst burden'd For pain and toil to cease; Come, Prince of Life and Glory, Bring universal peace.

CHORUS.

He's coming by and by, He's coming by and by, The night of sin is ending, The morning draweth nigh; He's coming by and by, He's coming by and by, The night of sin is ending, The morning draweth nigh.

Copyright, 1894, W. S. Weeden.

154. God's Love so Full and Free.

FRANCES R. HAVERGAL.   W. S. WEEDEN.

1. I know I love Thee bet-ter, Lord, Than a-ny earth-ly joy! For Thou hast giv-en me the peace Which noth-ing can de-stroy.
2. I know that Thou art near-er still Than a-ny earth-ly throng; And sweet-er is the thought of Thee Than a-ny love-ly song.
3. Thou hast put glad-ness in my heart; Then well may I be glad! With-out the se-cret of Thy love I could not but be sad.
4. O Sa-viour pre-cious Saviour, mine! What will thy presence be, If such a life of joy can crown My walk on earth with Thee.

CHORUS.

The half has never yet been told, Of love so full and free!
              yet been told,   full and free!

The half has never yet been told, The blood—it cleanseth me!
              yet been told,   cleanseth me!

Copyright, 1896, by W. S. WEEDEN.

156. Complete Surrender.

FRANCIS RIDLEY HAVERGAL.   W. S. WEEDEN.

1. Take my life, and let it be Con-se-crat-ed, Lord, to thee; Take my hands and let them move At the im-pulse of thy love.
2. Take my feet, and let them be Swift and beau-ti-ful for thee; Take my voice and let me sing Al-ways, on-ly, for my King.
3. Take my lips, and let them be, Filled with mes-sag-es for thee; Take my sil-ver and my gold,— Not a mite would I with-hold.
4. Take my moments and my days, Let them flow in end-less praise; Take my in-tel-lect, and use Ev-'ry power as thou shalt choose.

CHORUS.

{ All is on the al-tar, Lord, for Thee, } O bap-
{ Un-derneath the blood of Cal-va - - - ry. }
tise me now, While at Thy feet I bow, Let Thy Spir-it fall on me.

1 Take my will, and make it thine,
  It shall be no longer mine;
  Take my heart,—it is thine own,—
  It shall be thy royal throne.

6 Take my love,—my Lord, I pour
  At thy feet its treasure-store!
  Take myself, and I will be
  Ever, only, all for thee!

Copyright, 1896, by W. S. WEEDEN.

I am Coming to the Cross.

Rev. Wm. McDonald.   John vi. 37.   Wm. G. Fischer. By per.

1. I am com-ing to the cross; I am poor, and weak, and blind;
2. Long my heart has sighed for thee, Long has e-vil reigned within;
3. Here I give my all to thee, Friends, and time, and earthly store;

Cho.—I am trust-ing, Lord, in thee, Blest Lamb of Cal-va-ry;

I am count-ing all but dross, I shall full sal-va-tion find.
Je-sus sweet-ly speaks to me,— "I will cleanse you from all sin."
Soul and bo-dy thine to be,— Whol-ly thine for ev-er-more.

Humbly at thy cross I bow, Save me, Je-sus, save me now.

4 In thy promises I trust,
Now I feel the blood applied:
I am prostrate in the dust,
I with Christ am crucified.

5 Jesus comes! he fills my soul!
Perfected in him I am;
I am every whit made whole:
Glory, glory to the Lamb.

At the Fountain.

Old Melody.

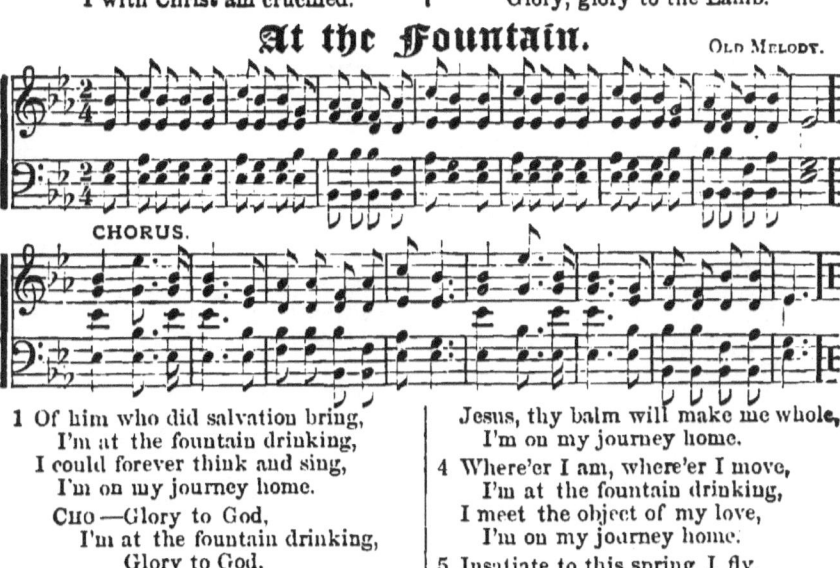

CHORUS.

1 Of him who did salvation bring,
I'm at the fountain drinking,
I could forever think and sing,
I'm on my journey home.

Cho—Glory to God,
I'm at the fountain drinking,
Glory to God,
I'm on my journey home.

2 Ask but his grace and lo! 'tis given,
I'm at the fountain drinking,
Ask and he turns your hell to heaven,
I'm on my journey home.

3 Tho' sin and sorrow wound my soul,
I'm at the fountain drinking,
Jesus, thy balm will make me whole,
I'm on my journey home.

4 Where'er I am, where'er I move,
I'm at the fountain drinking,
I meet the object of my love,
I'm on my journey home.

5 Insatiate to this spring I fly,
I'm at the fountain drinking,
I drink and yet am ever dry,
I'm on my journey home.

Cho.—Glory to God,
I'm at the fountain drinking,
Glory to God,
My soul is satisfied.

www.ingramcontent.com/pod-product-compliance
Lightning Source LLC
Chambersburg PA
CBHW030256170426
43202CB00009B/760